LET'S GO SOUL WINNING

Practical Principles in Soul Winning

BY

DR. DAVID N. SMELTZ SR.

Let's Go Soul Winning

All rights reserved. No part of this publication may be reproduced or stored in a retrieval system, transmitted in any form or by any means- electronic, mechanical, photocopy, recording or any other except for brief quotations in printed reviews without the prior permission of the author and publisher.

His Word of Truth Publication
116 Sweet Hills Drive
Amherst, VA, 24521

Copyright © 2014 David N. Smeltz His Word of Truth Ministry
All rights reserved.

ISBN-13: 978-1500404451

ISBN-10: 1500404454

INTRODUCTION

First, let me say thank you to the many individuals who have written materials on this subject. When I was in Bible College, I worked with Dr. J. O. Grooms as an associate for my Christian service. One of the things Dr Grooms stressed was scripture is what leads a person to Christ. We had to memorize several books of scripture designed to win someone to Christ. The little red book became my second Bible, as it was full of scripture. (Treasure Path to Soul Winning) Before we could witness we had to memorize every page in that book. This book contains the opinions from many who were great soul winners and the methods they used. I have tried to make this book as simple as possible. Originality is not the concept and I can take no credit for the illustrations and some of great concepts in this book for they have been passed down from generation to generation by great men of God. All of these men believed the Bible from cover to cover witnessed to thousands who came to Christ through door to door witnessing. Before the Jehovah Witness were around men went from house to house. **Acts 20:20 (KJV)**

[20] *And* how I kept back nothing that was profitable *unto you*, but have shewed you, and have taught you publickly, and from house to house, The church grows through sharing the Gospel with others. It is what the Bible teaches. The great Commission **Matthew 28:19-20 (KJV)** [19] Go ye therefore, and teach all nations, baptizing them in the name of the Father, and of the Son, and of the Holy Ghost: [20] Teaching them to observe all things whatsoever I have commanded you: and, lo, I am with you alway, *even* unto the end of the world. Amen. Keys on two words GO and teach...The going is sharing the Gospel and the teaching is discipleship. For over forty years, I have shared the Gospel with thousands around the world. Only the Lord knows the number of people who accepted Christ as Lord and Savior. The greatest Joy the believer has is to tell someone about what Christ has done on the cross of Calvary for there soul. I hope many will teach others how to be a soul winner will use this little book. My ultimate goal in these last days is for many to come to Christ. Please pass this book on to others.

David N Smeltz

Forward

A few years ago, we came into contact and became friends with Dr and Mrs. Smeltz. Our first time together was in our ministry as missionaries in the Philippines. Our ministry is centered around pastor training and church planting. Initially I was curious to see how Dr. Smeltz would impact our students and pastors.

On his trip to be with us in the Philippines, we planned several weeks of activities, including a trip to Cambodia and Vietnam, where he had served in the USA military in the fighting there. We visited several missionaries and ministries in those countries. In the Philippines, there was teaching and preaching activities in our Bible College and preaching in several churches. It was a blessing to see a man who is knowledgeable of scripture and how it applies in the world today. I was satisfied to see that he is very capable of expressing that knowledge, which he does in this book.

This easy to read book contains much information in the area of soul winning and all is valuable. Whether the reader is a new Christian or a person who has been saved for many years, this book is an important read. It will not only challenge a Christian to get involved in the activity of talking to people about salvation, but it can help the soul-winner with very effective methods when speaking with a variety of cultures and religions in our world today. The entire book is effective and full of scripture to verify the training proposed by Dr. Smeltz.

Dennis Ebert
Missionary to the Filipino People.
Philippines

TABLE OF CONTENTS

CHAPTER 1

Soul Winning Made Easy

THE VALUE OF A SOUL

How can we compute the value of a soul?

A STRIKING EXAMPLE

CHAPTER 2

THE FITNESS OF THE WORKER

CHAPTER 3

THE PLACE OF PRAYER IN SOUL-WINNING

CHAPTER 4

DO'S AND DON'TS FOR THE SOUL-WINNER

CHAPTER 5

AN OLD TESTAMENT ILLUSTRATION AND A NEW TESTAMENT EXAMPLE

CHAPTER 6

THE NEW TESTAMENT EXAMPLE

CHAPTER 7

THE APPROACH

THE DIAGNOSIS

CHAPTER 8

CONVERTED PERSONS.

CHAPTER 9

UNCONVERTED PERSONS

WHAT IT IS TO BELIEVE

CHAPTER 10

THE INDIFFERENT OR CARELESS

OBJECTIONS BASED ON THE INCONSISTENCIES OF CHRISTIANS.

CHAPTER 11

PERSONAL DIFFICULTIES

CHAPTER 12

WORKING AMONG FALSE CULTS
    ROMAN CATHOLICISM
    UNITARIANISM

How to lead a Muslim to Christ
    CHRISTIAN SCIENCE
    UNIVERSALISTS
    JEWS
    Russellism or Millenial Dawn, or JEHOVAH'S WITNESSES
    SPIRITISM
    THEOSOPHY
    SEVENTH DAY ADVENTISM
    MISCELLANEOUS SUGGESTIONS

CHAPTER 13

TRACT DISTRIBUTION
  A CONSECRATED PEN

CHAPTER 14

Follow Up

INSTRUCTION FOR CONVERTS

CLASS LESSONS

INTRODUCTION

LESSON 1

Soul Winning Made Easy

THE VALUE OF A SOUL

How can we compute the value of a soul?

A STRIKING EXAMPLE

LESSON 2

THE FITNESS OF THE WORKER

LESSON 3

THE PLACE OF PRAYER IN SOUL-WINNING

LESSON 4

DO'S AND DON'TS FOR THE SOUL-WINNER

LESSON 5

AN OLD TESTAMENT ILLUSTRATION AND A NEW TESTAMENT EXAMPLE

LESSON 6

THE NEW TESTAMENT EXAMPLE

LESSON 7

THE APPROACH

THE DIAGNOSIS

LESSON 8

CONVERTED PERSONS.

LESSON 9

UNCONVERTED PERSONS

WHAT IT IS TO BELIEVE

LESSON 10

THE INDIFFERENT OR CARELESS

OBJECTIONS BASED ON THE INCONSISTENCIES OF CHRISTIANS.

LESSON 11

PERSONAL DIFFICULTIES

LESSON 12

WORKING AMONG FALSE CULTS
   ROMAN CATHOLICISM
   UNITARIANISM

How to lead a Muslim to Christ
   CHRISTIAN SCIENCE
   UNIVERSALISTS
   JEWS
   Russellism or Millenial Dawn, or JEHOVAH'S WITNESSES
   SPIRITISM
   THEOSOPHY
   SEVENTH DAY ADVENTISM
   MISCELLANEOUS SUGGESTIONS

LESSON 13

TRACT DISTRIBUTION
   A CONSECRATED PEN

LESSON 14

Follow Up

INSTRUCTION FOR CONVERTS

ABOUT THE AUTHOR

Chapter 1

Soul Winning Made Easy

THE VALUE OF A SOUL

How can we compute the value of a soul?

It is so important to understand the value of a soul. God made man for worship and this means He loves every living soul. **John 3:16 (KJV)**
[16] For God so loved the world, that he gave his only begotten Son, that whosoever believeth in him should not perish, but have everlasting life.

1. **BY ITS NATURE AND ORIGIN** Man was made in the image of God, and into him was breathed the breath of God. Man is an immortal being.

2. **BY ITS POWERS AND CAPACITIES**

    The capacities of a human being, even in this life, seem almost limitless--but, alas, they have been prostituted to base uses in the service of the usurper. However, man is still capable of fellowship with God--the highest privilege conceivable to the mind of a human being.

3. **BY THE DURATION OF ITS <u>E</u>XISTENCE**

The human soul exists eternally, and either in bliss or in woe

2 Corinthians 4:18 (KJV)
[18] While we look not at the things which are seen, but at the things which are not seen: for the things which are seen *are* temporal; but the things which are not seen *are* eternal.

1 Corinthians 15:53 (KJV)
[53] For this corruptible must put on incorruption, and this mortal *must* put on immortality.

Romans 8:11 (KJV)
[11] But if the Spirit of him that raised up Jesus from the dead dwell in you, he that raised up Christ from the dead shall also quicken your mortal bodies by his Spirit that dwelleth in you.

Jude 1:7 (KJV)
[7] Even as Sodom and Gomorrha, and the cities about them in like manner, giving themselves over to fornication, and going after strange flesh, are set forth for an example, suffering the vengeance of eternal fire.

2 Peter 3:6-7 (KJV)
[6] Whereby the world that then was, being overflowed with water, perished:
[7] But the heavens and the earth, which are now, by the same word are kept in store, reserved unto fire against

the day of judgment and perdition of ungodly men.
Matthew 25:46 (KJV)
^{46} And these shall go away into everlasting punishment: but the righteous into life eternal.

4. **BY THE COST OF ITS REDEMPTION** It required not shining silver or yellow gold to pay the price of man's redemption, but crimson drops of precious blood from the broken body of the Son of God. This makes even the meanest soul worth saving.

5. **BY THE STRUGGLE REQUIRED FOR ITS POSSESSION**

    Why is the unregenerate human soul the battleground of both God and the Devil: the one actuated by love, the other by hate, because both know and rightly appraise the possibilities for good and evil of only one human soul. No wonder souls are not lightly won, with such an adversary. If then a soul is of such surpassing value to save it, no expense is too large, no pain too agonizing, no trouble too great, no labor too hard.

    Impelled by a great passion for souls, Raymond Lull, first missionary to the Moslems, cried, "To Thee, O Lord, I offer myself, my wife, my children, and all that I possess." After many years of suffering and service, he became a martyr for his Lord. David Branierd, who died when little more than thirty, said: "I wanted to wear myself out in His service, for His glory. I cared not how or where I lived, or what hardships I went through so that I could but gain souls for Christ."

Such love has burned in the breasts of all great soul-winners. Their love for souls has been reckless and prodigal.

The Big Question, HOW MAY THIS "CONCERN" BE OBTAINED
- It is not a natural and inevitable product of the heart.
- It is not produced by a fresh resolution to be concerned about souls.
- It will be produced in the heart only by using the means adapted to stir up our minds on the subject. Paul's concern for souls, as one has said, sprang from a threefold conviction.

First, one great verity that all must face, the Great White Throne;

Second, one experience through which all men must pass is the resurrection either to life or to condemnation.

Third, one destiny toward which all things are moving--the great eternity.

We must cherish the slightest impression of the Spirit; take the Bible and go over the passages that show the condition of lost sinners. Dr. Wilbur Chapman suggests "Take your New Testament and go quietly alone and read a sentence like this: 'He that believeth not is condemned already.' Then sit and think about it for ten minutes. Put your boy over against it-- your girl, your wife, your husband, yourself. Then take this: 'He that hath not the Son of God, hath not life, but the wrath of God abideth on him.' I know that a soul thus burdened generally gains its desire."

Charles G. Finney urges the seeker after this "concern" to "look as it were, through a telescope into Hell, and hear their groans; then turn the glass upward and look into Heaven and see the saints there in their white robes, and hear them sing the song of redeeming love; and ask yourself: **'Is it possible that I should prevail with God to elevate the sinner there?'** Do this, and if you are not a wicked man, you will soon have as much of the spirit of prayer as your body can sustain."

Lord Crucified, give me a love like Thine,

Help me to win the dying souls of men.

Lord, keep my heart in closest touch with Thine

And give me love, pure Calvary love,

To bring the lost to Thee.

A STRIKING EXAMPLE

A most striking example of the urge to win souls triumphing over even death is that of John Harper, a Baptist minister of London, who was lost with the TITANIC. At a conference held in the city of Hamilton, Ontario, Canada, a man rose and gave the following testimony: *"Four years ago, when I left England on board the TITANIC, I was a careless, godless sinner. I was in this condition on the night when the terrible catastrophe took place. Very soon, with hundreds more, I found myself struggling in the cold, dark waters of the Atlantic. I caught hold of something and clung to it for dear life. The wail of awful distress from the perishing all around was ringing in my* ears, when there floated nearby me a man who, too, seemed to be clinging to something. He called to me: 'Is your soul saved?' I replied 'No, it is not.' 'Then,' said he, 'Believe on the Lord Jesus Christ, and thou shalt be saved.' We drifted apart for a few minutes, and then we seemed to be driven together once more. 'Is your soul saved?' Again, he cried out. 'I fear it is not,' I replied. 'Then if you will but believe on the Lord Jesus Christ your soul shall be saved,' was his further message of intense appeal to me. Again, we were separated by the rolling currents. I heard him call out this message to others as they sank beneath the waters into eternity. There and then, with two miles of water beneath me, in my desperation I cried unto Christ to save me. I believed upon Him and I was saved. In a few minutes I heard this man of God say: 'I'm going down, I'm going down ' then: 'No, no, I'm going UP.' That man was John Harper."

I. ABSENCE OF CONCEPTION OF THE VALUE OF A SOUL

Upon our conception of the value of the object to be won will depend the strenuousness of our labors for their salvation. "Is it really worth inconveniencing ourselves and interfering with our own enjoyment to save souls?" we ask. Let us endeavor to arrive at some true estimate of the value of a soul. A man will work harder to recover diamonds than gravel. Why? Because they are of so much greater value. And so with the souls of men. Christ conceived the human soul to be of such transcendent value that He gladly exchanged the shining courts of glory for a life of poverty, suffering, shame and death, rather than that it should perish. He placed the world and all it could offer in the one scale and a human soul in the other, and declared that the scale went down on the side of the soul.

Chapter 2

THE FITNESS OF THE WORKER

"I have come to the conclusion that everyone is not called to be a soul-winner," said a young man recently. That would make a pleasant hearing, indeed, for those who desire to shirk soul-winning work, but, unfortunately for them the young man's conclusion was erroneous! He would find it exceedingly difficult to substantiate his case from Scripture. So long as the Great Commission is unrevoked, so long as "Go YE into all the world and preach the gospel to every creature" remains in the Sacred Volume, there rests on each the personal responsibility of endeavoring to win souls for Christ, and for this he requires a special fitness.

I.   **AN UNWAVERING PURPOSE**

Since this work is of such supreme importance, the wise soul-winner will seek the very highest qualifications for the work. All great soul-winners have been impelled by such a purpose. The gifted American evangelist, Dr. Nettleton, whose labors in America so often culminated in revival; one time put the question to himself: "What will I wish I had done with my life thousands of years hence?" His answer to that question resulted in his devoting himself throughout life to the work of seeking to win souls.

Not many hours after his own conversion as a result of receiving a letter of appeal from his intimate friend, that keen soul-winner, Dr. Clay Trumbull, formed a great life resolve. Let me give you his own words: "The purpose I formed was, as an imperative duty, not to fail in my Christian life in confessing Christ to others. I determined that as I loved Christ, and as Christ loved souls, I would press Christ on the individual soul, so that none who was in the proper sphere of my individual responsibility or influence should lack the opportunity of meeting the question, whether or not they would individually trust and follow Christ. The resolve I made was that **WHENEVER I WAS IN SUCH INTIMACY WITH A SOUL AS TO BE JUSTIFIED IN CHOOSING MY THEME OF CONVERSATION, THE THEME OF THEMES SHOULD HAVE PROMINENCE BETWEEN US,** so that I might learn his need, and if possible meet it." This life-resolve was faithfully adhered to for more than fifty years. Who can estimate its results? Have you made such a resolve, my reader? If not, will you fall on your knees as you read and make it now?

When Dr. Lyman Beecher lay dying, a ministerial friend said to him: "Dr. Beecher, you know a great deal; tell us what is the greatest of all things." The dying preacher replied, "It is not theology; it is not controversy; **IT IS TO SAVE SOULS.**"

If such be true, shall we not place ourselves in the hands of the Master Soul-winner, saying: "Master, make me, with all my handicaps and disabilities, a fisher of men"?

He will surely respond, as He did to failing Peter: **"Follow me, and I WILL make YOU a fisher of men."**

II. AN UNASSAILABLE ASSURANCE OF HIS OWN SALVATION

This is another indispensable qualification of the soul-winner. Suppose one on whom you were pressing the claims of Christ turned to you with the question, "Are you absolutely certain you yourself are saved?" What would you answer? Could you ring out an unhesitating, "Yes, thank God, I am"? Our Lord said, "We speak that we do KNOW" (Jo 3:11). All around us are men and women, old and young, who are longing to find someone who knows, who can speak on this subject with conviction and authority. They are tired of negations, doubts, and speculations. They have enough of their own. If you do not possess this unshakable assurance, search the Word of God until you "KNOW that you HAVE eternal life" (1Jo 5:13).

Many truly converted people know nothing of a settled assurance of salvation because the life has never been fully yielded to Christ. The writer, although born again, was often tormented by doubts until the age of about twenty he wholly surrendered to the Lordship of Christ. Since that hour, no doubt has found even temporary lodgment in his heart.

III. A WORKING KNOWLEDGE OF THE SCRIPTURES

The soul-winner must not only believe the Bible, but know and study it. Other knowledge is doubtless valuable, but a knowledge of the Bible is of paramount importance. Nothing can take its place. Every soul-winner must acquire as speedily as possible, first, a general knowledge of the Bible, its main contents and teachings, and then how its message can best be applied in this work, for the Bible is the soul-winner's only kit of tools. Just as the physician does not give the same prescription for each case, so the same verse will not cause the light to break on every soul. Hence the necessity of being familiar with all the Scriptures which are relevant to soul-winning work. That worker will be most successful whose mind is most liberally stored with apt and suitable Scriptures.

Murray McCheyne used to say: "It is not our comment on the Word that saves, but the Word itself." When argument and persuasion fail to produce conviction or to bring the soul to decision, the intelligent use of the "Sword of the Spirit" often produces the desired result. How frequently one has seen opposition silenced and interest awakened by the sledgehammer blows of the Word when wielded in the power of the Spirit. It is the Word which the Spirit uses to convict of sin (Ac 2:37), and to reveal the way of salvation (2Ti 3:15). It is with the Bible that objections and excuses can be met, or modern heresies exposed; therefore the soul-winner MUST be a man of the BOOK if he is to know success.

To summarize in the words of Dr. Torrey:

1. A soul-winner should know how to use his Bible so as to show others their need of a Saviour.

2. To show them that Jesus Christ is just the Saviour they need.

3. To show them how to make Him their own Saviour

4. To deal with difficulties which hinder them from doing this.

To these we would add:

5   The soul-winner should have a living and active faith in the power of the Word of God to save the most difficult case.

One of the first students of Spurgeon's College came to him with the lament: "I have been preaching now for some months and I do not think I have had a single conversion." "And do you expect that the Lord is going to bless you and save souls every time you open your mouth?" said Spurgeon. "No, sir," he replied. "Well, then, that is why you do not get souls saved," was the rejoinder. "If you had believed, the Lord would have given you the blessing." Our faith in the Word and power of God must be such that we will expect God to save souls through our instrumentality.

IV. A HABITUALLY PRAYERFUL ATTITUDE

How many possibilities of error there are in such a work as this! The worker must be led as to which direction to take, and to whom to speak; to rightly diagnose the case, and to prescribe the appropriate remedy. Well might he cry with Paul: "Who is sufficient for these things?" Only as the heart is constantly being lifted to God in prayer for promised wisdom will he be preserved from blundering. He must pray before, during, and after his work.

It was because Philip was a man of prayer and in touch with God that he was guided to that seeking soul in the most unlikely spot, the desert.

I remember hearing the story of a blind man physically but exceptionally keen-sighted spiritually, had on many occasions unsuccessfully endeavored to bring the light of salvation to an ignorant old woman who lived nearby. At last he come to his wits' end and left the room to pray. In his prayer he told the Lord that he had done all he could. Was there no Scripture applicable to this case? Then a verse came to his mind: "Ye shall be my sons and daughters, saith the Lord Almighty." "But, Lord," he protested, "that has nothing to do with salvation." Try as he would, he could get no other message, so he quoted this verse to his friend. "Does it say that?" She eagerly asked; "I thought it was all for men. 'If any MAN thirsts,' but this verse says: 'Ye shall be MY sons and DAUGHTERS.'" Merely human wisdom would never have suggested this verse as the solution of the old woman's difficulties, but through prayer, he was given the unerring counsel of the Spirit of God. He often used this incident as an illustration of the absolute necessity of depending on the Spirit of God for the "word in season."

It has been said that for the personal worker the rule of the road is: "Go as you pray, and pray as you go."

V. A LOVINGLY TACTFUL APPROACH

Tact has been defined as the art of putting ourselves in the place of others so that we may know their needs and supply them, their prejudices, and conciliate them. It is an intuitive perception of what is proper or fitting; the mental ability of saying and doing the right thing at the right time, so as not to unnecessarily offend or anger. This qualification is sadly often conspicuous by its absence, and the worker spoils the very work about which he is so concerned.

On one occasion, D. L. Moody, without mentioning religion, played tennis a whole afternoon with a young fellow who was expecting to be button-holed at once, and was ready to resent any personal dealing. It was after he had won the young fellow to himself that he won him for Christ. He exhibited true tact.

Tact is not always a natural gift, but may in measure be acquired by observation, study, and prayer. We should try to imagine how we would feel and react if we were in the position of our "prospect," and act accordingly. Much is gained if we can make people feel at ease with us.

The story is told of a gentleman crossing the ocean who was distressed by the profanity of several men of the party. Finally, he said to them: "Gentlemen, I believe all of you are Englishmen, and if so, you believe in fair play, do you not?"

"Certainly, that is characteristic of Britons everywhere."

"Well, gentlemen, I notice that you have been indulging in a good deal of profanity, and I think it is my turn to swear next. Isn't that fair?"

"Of course it is," said the others.

"Very well, remember that you are not to swear again till I have had my turn."

"But you will not take your turn."   "I certainly

From the study of the biographies of all great soul-winners will emerge the fact that in each life there came a crisis, a new and fuller surrender to the Lord, and an enduement with power from on high for the discharge of the ministry entrusted to them. They learned to recognize in the Holy Spirit Himself their power for service. If you know little or nothing of His empowering in your experience, do not rest until it becomes a vital reality in your life. (Read #Lu 24:49 Ac 1:8,10 1Co 2:4, etc.)

Will just as soon as I see a real occasion for it."

All this was done in a playful way, but the result of his tactful approach was that they kept their profanity bottled up for the rest of the voyage.

V. THE ENDUEMENT WITH POWER

Although we have placed this qualification last in order, it is not because it is least in importance. Without it, one may have formed an unwavering purpose, enjoy an unassailable assurance, possess a working knowledge of the Scriptures, be very prayerful, and exercise much tact, and yet not be a successful soul-winner. With it, the value of all this equipment is immeasurably enhanced. I remember Dr. Jack Hyles of the great First Baptist Church at pastors conferences would say, "Pray for Power" and in my Bible on the first page, "it says, "Pray for Power."

Ponder the marvelous transformation in Peter after he had been "endued with power from on high." He preached with a passion, a fearlessness, a convicting power of which he was previously incapable. His words from then on left saving impressions on the minds of his hearers. Then, and then only, did he become the great "fisher of men." Seek and obtain this inducement, without which your most earnest endeavors will prove abortive.

I am trusting Thee for power, Thine can never fail,

Words which Thou Thyself shalt give me must prevail: Strenuousness of our labors for their salvation. "Is it really worth inconveniencing ourselves and interfering with our own enjoyment to save souls?" we ask. Let us endeavor to arrive at some true estimate of the value of a soul. A man will work harder to recover diamonds than gravel. Why? Because they are of so much greater value. And so with the souls of men. Christ conceived the human soul to be of such transcendent value that He gladly exchanged the shining courts of glory for a life of poverty, suffering, shame and death, rather than that it should perish. He placed the world and all it could offer in the one scale and a human soul in the other, and declared that the scale went down on the side of the soul.

Chapter 3

THE PLACE OF PRAYER IN SOUL-WINNING

HE IS COUNTING ON YOU

He is counting on you! On a love that will share In His burden of prayer, for the souls He has bought With His life-blood, and sought Through His sorrow and pain to win "home" yet again. He is counting on you! If you fail Him--

What Next? "PRAYER"

The worker whose supreme desire and passion is to be used in co-operation with the Holy Spirit in the winning of men to Christ, must master in some degree the holy art of intercession. If the Master wept and prayed over lost souls, then His servant must do the same. Prayer must ever occupy a pre-eminent place in the soul-winner's program, for the salvation of the soul is not a human, but a divine work. Only through prayer can the power of God be released.

If prayer, then, occupies so important a place, it follows that whatever hinders us in its exercise must be sacrificed. Any price is worth paying which will make us more powerful in prayer. If God is to answer our prayers, **WE MUST BE SURE THAT WE ARE STANDING ON PRAYING GROUND.** The psalmist warns: "If I regard [cling to] iniquity in my heart, the Lord WILL NOT HEAR ME" (Ps 66:18), let alone answer me. Before we are on true praying ground, we must have renounced every sin about which the Holy Spirit has convicted us. Have you done this, or is there a controversy between your soul and God. You will know when the last thing has been dealt with. You will feel the cleansing power of the blood of Christ.

Then it is necessary that we have a **HEART AT LEISURE FROM ITSELF** and its own concerns, a heart that is able to bear the burden of souls and to travail for them in birth until the new life is implanted. Listen to the apostle Paul as he prays, and note how his prayers are all for others. "I could wish that I myself were accursed from Christ for my brethren, my kinsmen according to the flesh" (Ro 9:3). Mark Epaphras, "always laboring fervently ... in prayers" (Col 4:12). Hear Count Zinzendorf as he prays for a few girls ranging in age from ten to thirteen whose spiritual education has become his care. "He observed that though their demeanor was blameless, and their intellectual grasp of the truth was satisfactory, yet no evidence of a heart knowledge of God appeared among them. This weighed on his soul and led him to earnest intercession for them. Cultured, wealthy young man that he was, he was not above taking thought for the spiritual welfare of a few girls. More intense grew his concern, culminating at last in a season of such truly energized prayer as produced a most extraordinary effect." The blessing he desired for his class came, and much more too, for this was the beginning of the mighty work among the Moravians, which bore fruit in their marvelous missionary enterprise.

The soul-winner's prayer will be first for himself, and then for the soul to be won. For himself he will need to pray a threefold prayer.

FIRST: for MORAL COURAGE TO SPEAK FOR CHRIST WHEN OPPORTUNITY OFFERS

In the world, which crucified Christ, it will never be easy to speak for Him. To some, the fear of man is an almost insuperable barrier. Is it boldness you need? Then do as the disciples did--pray! "Grant unto thy servants that with all boldness they may speak thy word ... And they spake the word with boldness" (Ac 4:29-31). "I can do ALL THINGS through Christ which strengtheneth me" (Php 4:13). You will be able, after prayer, to do what you never could have done without it.

SECOND, FOR GUIDANCE AS TO WHOM TO APPROACH To speak to men indiscriminately and without inspiration and guidance is often hurtful both to the worker and to those whom he addresses. It goes without saying that God does not expect us to speak to everyone we meet, although He does expect us to be willing so to do. Dr. F. B. Meyer used to feel constantly burdened in regard to speaking to everyone he met, until he made it a matter of prayer that God would show him the ones to whom to speak. The case of Philip the evangelist is an outstanding example of this. (Ac 8:26.) There are many souls with whom we can come into contact, for whom God has no message at that moment. If we cultivate the habit of constantly looking to the Lord for instructions, He will guide us with His eye as to when to speak and when to keep silent.

Dr. Torrey made a practice of sitting in a double railway seat, and then prayed that God would bring to his seat the person whom he could help.

THIRD, FOR GUIDANCE AS TO WHAT TO SAY Let the reader remember that every soul-winner was once as inexperienced as he is. If God is calling you to speak to someone, then surely you can trust Him for the message. He knows what each case needs, and has given the Holy Spirit for the very purpose of bringing the right Scriptures to your remembrance. Trust Him to do it. "He shall bring all things to your remembrance, whatsoever I have said unto you" (Jo 14:26).

The worker's prayer for the soul to be won will also be threefold.

FIRST: THAT ANY INDIFFERENCE OR HOSTILITY MAY BE BROKEN DOWN AND AN OPENING MADE FOR DELIVERING THE MESSAGE OF SALVATION.

Unless the Spirit of God precedes the worker, he will try in vain to storm the citadel of the soul. Persistent, believing prayer has often broken down the most determined opposition.

SECOND: THAT THE SOIL OF THE HEART MAY BE PREPARED FOR THE SOWING OF THE SEED

This again is the work of the Spirit of God. "When he, the Spirit of truth is come, he shall convict the world of sin, of righteousness and of judgment" (Jo 16:8). He does His work of conviction in answer to prayer.

THIRD: THAT THE SOUL MAY BE LIBERATED FROM THE POWER OF SATAN.

It is just here that the real battle is fought. Prayer of this kind is a spiritual warfare. Satan, the strong man armed of Mt 12:29, has bound every son of Adam, and contests their deliverance every inch of the way. It is by believing prayer alone that the strong man can be bound and souls delivered. "They overcame him by the blood of the Lamb and by the word of their testimony" (Rev 12:11). *The prayer warrior must learn how to plead the victory of Calvary, for the blood of the Lamb has forever broken the power of the Devil,* and robbed him of his prey. "Real prayer," says Gordon Watt, "is opposing a great spiritual force to the onslaught of evil, and asking God to put into operation the work done by His Son on the cross, which was not only the redemption of man, but the defeat of the prince of this world." Plead the blood of the Lamb for the liberation of the soul for whom you pray.

Our praying is likely to be futile unless it is DEFINITE IN ITS AIM. The marksman is aiming at one spot in all the wide world. After he has shot, he knows whether or not he has hit it. Our prayers should be of a similar order. They should be so definite that we shall know whether or not they have been answered. We must pray for definite souls. But for which souls? Here again the Holy Spirit comes to our aid.

OUR PETITIONS SHOULD BE SPIRIT-TAUGHT. As we wait before God, He will burden our hearts for certain souls who are within the sphere of our influence. In Dr. Torrey's first pastorate, God laid on his heart in this way two persons. He prayed for them throughout his pastorate, but neither was converted. For some years he kept on praying for them daily, and when later conducting a mission in that city both accepted Christ the same night. His was a Spirit-taught petition. How appropriate are the words of Scripture: "We know not what we should pray for as we ought, but the Spirit helpeth our infirmities" (Ro 8:26).

Then in addition, our praying should be SYSTEMATIC. Too often, we pray haphazardly for whatever comes into the mind.

"The Lord is a God of system" (Is 30:18). His children should be like Him. System in praying will help to beget that **PERSEVERANCE** which is so often conspicuous by its absence from our prayers. We pray and run away. "Foolish boys that knock at a door in wantonness," said the old Puritan, "will not stay till someone cometh to open to them, but a man that hath business will knock and knock again until his call is answered." "Knock, and it shall be opened unto you, for ... to him that knocketh [knocks, and] [keeps on knocking] **IT SHALL BE OPENED**" (Lu 11:9,10). Let us not hang up the receiver before the answer comes over the heavenly wires. **"Men ought always to pray AND NOT TO FAINT" (Lu 18:1).**

Nevertheless, apart from a **BELIEVING HEART** all the foregoing conditions may be complied with, and yet no answer be received. "He that cometh to God **MUST BELIEVE**" (Heb 11:6). "But let him ask in faith, **NOTHING WAVERING**, for he that wavereth ... let not that man think that he shall receive ANYTHING of the Lord" (Ja 1:6,7). Count on God's good faith. Do not grieve and dishonor Him through disbelieving Him. "He is faithful that promised." Expect Him to do the unexpected.

There is no method which is of greater help in securing definiteness of aim, system, and perseverance in prayer than the use of the "Throne of Grace Book," of the One by One Band. It consists almost entirely of blank pages on which are entered the names of people for whom the Spirit has impressed the worker to pray, space being left for the insertion of the date of answer. Anyone can make his own book of remembrance, and keep these souls constantly before the Lord in prayer. Begin at once. You will find that very soon, your praying will prepare the way for witnessing, and you will have the surpassing joy of entering the date of answer opposite some of the names.

Prayer is God's mightiest instrument in the salvation of souls, and it is to be doubted if any soul is saved apart from the believing prayer of some saint. Writing of his own conversion, Dr. J. Hudson Taylor said: "Little did I know at that time what was going on in the heart of my dear mother, 70 or 80 miles away. She rose from the dinner table that afternoon with an intense yearning for her boy's conversion, and feeling that a special opportunity was afforded her of pleading with God on my behalf, she went to her room and turned the key in the door, resolved not to leave that spot until her prayers were answered. Hour after hour, that dear mother pleaded for me, until at length she could pray no longer, but was constrained to praise God for that which His Spirit had taught her was already accomplished--the conversion of her only son.

"When our dear mother came home a fortnight later, I was the first to meet her at the door, and to tell her I had such glad news to give. I can almost feel that dear mother's arms around my neck as she pressed me to her bosom and said: 'I know, my boy; I have been rejoicing for a fortnight in the glad tidings you have to tell me.'

"'Why,' I asked in surprise, 'has Amelia broken her promise? She said she would tell no one.'

"My dear mother assured me that it was not from any human source that she had learned the tidings, and went on to tell the little incident above. You will agree with me that it would be strange indeed if I were not a believer in the power of prayer."

LORD, TEACH US TO PRAY

Chapter 4

DO'S AND DON'TS FOR THE SOUL-WINNER

The aim of these studies is eminently practical. They shall have failed of their purpose if many readers are not stirred to engage in this most fascinating and fruitful form of Christian service. The need of a genuine concern for souls and the necessary qualifications of a soul-winner, have been passed under review. The next step is to be found in 2Sa 3:18: "Now then, do it." The art can be learned in no other way.

"Soul-saving is a divine art," says Dr. T. C. Horton. "Men are not born soul-savers, but are made. There is a widespread misapprehension in the minds of most Christians concerning responsibility for this work. Christians seem to think that **SOME** people are called to this work, but that the obligation is not universal; that it is work which one **MAY DO** or not do, as they choose. This is false, unscriptural, and illogical. Soul saving is the greatest work in the world, and is committed to every believer. All may have the joy of doing it that **GIVE THEMSELVES** to it, and all who fail to do it are responsible to a holy trust, and will be the poorer throughout eternity." If this were true, now then, do it.

1. **DO BELIEVE GOD'S PROMISE OF WISDOM (Ja 1:5).**
Many hold back from this work because they feel so ill equipped to engage in it, and are sure that they will never succeed. But has the faithful God not said: "If any of you lack wisdom, let him ask of God, who giveth to all men liberally ... and it shall be given him"? Can you not trust Him to keep His word? Often stammering words, prompted by a genuine concern, achieve more than an eloquent discourse. Even if we seem to fail, God can bless our blunders as the following story shows.

Dr. L. G. Broughton once said to an ignorant member of his congregation: "Why don't you speak to someone about Jesus Christ?"

"I will," he said. He walked down the aisle and sat beside a brilliant young lawyer. "Do you want to go to Heaven when you die?" he commenced.

"I don't know whether I do or not," answered the man.

"All right, then, go to Hell." He rose and left him.

The lawyer was piqued, but the shaft went home. When visiting Dr. Broughton a few days later he confessed: "I hate to acknowledge it, but that remark of that blundering fool of yours kept ringing in my ears, and I could not get rid of it. At last I got down on my knees, and said: 'Lord, give me the faith of that blundering fool who made me so mad,' and **JESUS SAVED ME**."

They went together to the home of the "blundering fool," and, with tears streaming down his face; the lawyer wrung his hand, saying: "You are the man who led me to Christ."

I am not **COMMENDING** his method of approach, but I do contend that the result certainly atoned for his faulty method. Are you willing to be a blundering fool for Christ? Sometimes a direct approach will get results while beating around the bush takes longer. Dr. J.O. Grooms a dear friend who is in heaven had a direct approach. He always used scripture in his approach and was very successful as a soul winner.

2. **DO CLAIM DELIVERANCE FROM THE FEAR OF MAN.**

It is essential that the soul-winner should lose the fear of man. As a young convert, I met a man who was very bold in his soul winning efforts. One day, feeling my bondage to the fear of man, I ventured to ask him if he had always been bold in this work. He replied that he had been as timid as anyone, until one day he could stand it no longer. He fell on his knees with his Bible open at Ps 34:4: "I sought the Lord, and he heard me and **DELIVERED ME FROM ALL MY FEARS.**" "Lord, you did this for David," he prayed; "do it for me now." From that moment, his timidity was replaced by a holy boldness. So long as we are in bondage to the opinions of the world, our work will be circumscribed and hampered. There are many who fail to engage in aggressive soul winning through fear of being thought peculiar. You need to claim deliverance from this satanic fear. God will give a full deliverance to the most timid and fearful soul who dares to claim it.

3. **DO KEEP YOUR EYES OPEN FOR OPPORTUNITIES.**

I have found myself surrounded with opportunities **WHEN WILLING TO SEIZE THEM**, but when I was unwilling, no opportunities seemed to present themselves. Doubtless, there were just as many opportunities, but I was blind to them. We can be so occupied with what we consider "bigger things" that we neglect to speak to the store keeper, gas station worker bank clerk or person we work with everyday.

The following confession by a missionary secretary appeared some years ago in THE MISSIONARY REVIEW OF THE WORLD: "I was helping to get up a big Convention, and was full of enthusiasm over making the session a success. On the opening day, my aged father, who came as a delegate to the Convention, sat with me at luncheon at the hotel. He listened sympathetically to my glowing accounts of the great features that were to be. When I paused for breath, he leaned toward me and said, while his eye followed the stately movements of the head waiter: 'Daughter, I think that big head waiter over there is going to accept Jesus Christ. I've been talking to him about his soul' I almost gasped. I had been too busy planning for a great missionary convention. I had no time to think of the soul of the head waiter.

When we went out to my apartment, a Black man was washing the apartment windows. Jim was honest and trustworthy, and had been a most satisfactory helper in my home. Only a few moments passed before I heard my father talking earnestly with Jim about his personal salvation, and a swift accusation went to my heart as I realized that I had known Jim for years, and had never said a word to him of salvation.

"A carpenter came in to repair a door. I awaited his going with impatience to sign his work ticket, for my ardent soul longed to be back at my missionary task. Even as I waited, I heard my father talking with the man about the door he had just fixed, and then simply and naturally leading the conversation to the only door into the Kingdom of God.

"A Jew lives across the street. I had thought that possibly, I would call on the folks who lived in the neighborhood--some time--but I had my hands so full of missionary work the calls had never been made; but, as they met on the street, my father talked with my neighbor of the only Savior of the world.

"A friend took us out to ride. I waited for my father to get into the car, but in a moment, he was up beside the chauffeur, and in a few minutes I heard him talking earnestly with the man about the way of salvation. When we reached home, he said: 'You know, I was afraid I might never have another chance to speak to that man.'

"The wife of a prominent railway man took him out to ride in her elegant limousine. 'I am glad she asked me to go,' for it gave me an opportunity of talking with her about her salvation. I think no one had ever talked with her before.'

"Yet these opportunities had come to me also, and had passed by as ships in the night, while I strained my eyes to catch sight of a larger sail on a more distant horizon. I could but question my own heart whether my passion was for souls, or for success in getting up conventions."

Comment is needless. We are surrounded by opportunities--in our homes, in the church, in the Sunday school, among our friends, relatives, neighbors, employees, fellow workers, on trains or cars, in parks or on the streets, if only we are willing to avail ourselves of them. We need to improve your opportunities.

4 **DO PURPOSE TO WIN ONE SOUL.** You might well shrink from the task if you were asked to win twenty souls; but could you not win one. Have you ever honestly tried this? Do not say, "I can't!" for God never requires us to do something we cannot do. Ask the Lord to lay one soul upon your heart, and then lay yourself out to win that one. Incalculable possibilities lie in this purpose.

Dwight L. Moody, who later became the great evangelist, was reared in a Unitarian environment, went to Boston at an early age, was induced to join a Sunday school class, and was led to a definite acceptance of Christ through the faithful personal persuasion of the teacher of that class. When Andrew brought Peter to Jesus, he brought through Peter 3,000 souls on the day of Pentecost; and when Edward Kimball brought Moody to Jesus, he brought, through Moody, a million souls to Christ, and by that much moved the whole world Godward. One soul is worth it all, but infinite possibilities are wrapped up in **EVERY** soul.

Let's Go Soul Winning

But consider the negative side. Joseph Smith, who later became the leader of the Mormon Church, lived in a neglected home in a certain country community. A farmer on his way to church passed that home every Sunday, but he never asked the poor lad to accompany him, or even to attend Sunday school. The sad consequences of that failure will never be blotted out. Unnumbered lives have been blighted and homes ruined. Oh, the tragedy of failure!

In **EVERY** community there are potential Moody's, potential Surgeon's, and also, alas, POTENTIAL JOSEPH SMITHS! There may be one or the other IN YOUR OWN HOME, or in your neighbor's home. Dr. Jack Hyles was a bus kid. Jerry Falwell was the son of a bootlegger. Do seek to win at least one soul for your Lord.

In order to crystallize this purpose for you, will you, or will you not, here and now append your name to the following suggested pledge?

WIN ONE SOUL

I will seek, with God's help, to win one

Soul each year, and endeavor to get them

To do the same

Name ....

SOME DON'TS

Let's Go Soul Winning

1. **DON'T LET IT BE APPARENT THAT YOU ARE A PERSONAL WORKER.** Conceal your hook. If you are using tracts, hide them.

2. **DON'T ATTEMPT TO DEAL WITH MORE THAN ONE SOUL AT A TIME.** Get your "prospect" alone, or he will never open his heart to you and disclose his real difficulty.

3. **DON'T BE DRAWN INTO AN ARGUMENT.** you will most likely be side-tracked from your main objective if you do. Few have been argued into salvation. Duncan Mathieson tells how, in his unregenerate days, an earnest Christian used to speak to him about his soul. This friend was very staunch concerning his denominational tenets, and, in order to avoid a pointed talk about salvation, Mathieson used to attack his views on these matters, and the old man at once brought forth arguments to prove his views were right, and doubtless succeeded in defeating his opponent's arguments; but this was much to Mathieson's liking. He had escaped the personal talk about the condition of his soul. Keep your man pinned to his personal responsibility to Christ.

4. **DON'T ATTRACT ATTENTION TO YOURSELF** or your experience. Seek to attract souls to your Lord.

5. **DON'T MONOPOLIZE THE CONVERSATION.** If your man has a lot to say, give him a patient

hearing. You will be better able to deal with him if you know his viewpoint. He will come to an end of his talking sooner or later, and then your chance will come.

6. **DON'T AS A RULE DEAL WITH PERSONS OF THE OPPOSITE SEX.** If possible, pass them over to some worker of the same sex. It is not becoming for a young man or a young woman to be always looking for a person of the opposite sex to deal with.

7. **DON'T AS A RULE CHOOSE A PERSON MUCH YOUR SENIOR TO DEAL WITH** Of course, there are exceptions to both this and the previous "don't".

8. **DON'T RELY ON YOUR OWN ABILITY**, powers of persuasion, or knowledge of the Scriptures. Maintain an attitude of constant dependence on the Holy Spirit to wield His sword.

9. **DON'T MULTIPLY TEXTS AND ILLUSTRATIONS.** Have THREE or FOUR texts, which reveal the need and the remedy, with one or two pertinent illustrations. Answer difficulties from the Word rather than from your own experience.

10. **DON'T BE UNDULY FAMILIAR** with your inquirer. Avoid putting hand on shoulder or arm around him, as it sometimes arouses resentment.

11. **DON'T BECOME IMPATIENT** even if cause has been given. Return good for evil.

12. **DON'T BREAK IN WHEN SOMEONE ELSE IS DEALING WITH A SOUL.** Never interrupt at such a moment of crisis. You may feel you could do far better, and perhaps that is so, but this is not the time for you to do it. Do not even stand by. Similarly, do not allow others to interrupt you.

13. **DON'T HURRY OR DO SHODDY WORK.** "He that believeth shall not make haste." (Is 28:16).

14. **DON'T BE DISCOURAGED** by apparent failure. Pray and think over every case in which you fail, asking the Lord to show you how to deal with a similar case next time. Thus your failures may become stepping-stones. In any case, the Word of God never fails.

15. **DON'T FORGET** that your only weapons are "the Sword of the Spirit" (Ep 6:17); and the weapon of "all prayer" (Ep 6:18). Make full use of both.

The value of one soul, O Lord, Teach me to see; and as Thy Word Assures me of the awful fate Which doth the Christless soul await, Oh, may I wrestle and prevail With God and men, like Israel.

> *Give me Thy tenderness and tact, Guide every thought and word and act, And cause me so to do my part To reach the hard or longing heart, That men to Thee, O Christ, may turn, More of Thy tenderness to learn.*

--Estelle Edmeades

Chapter 5

AN OLD TESTAMENT ILLUSTRATION AND A NEW TESTAMENT EXAMPLE

My brother, I do not know how any Christian Service is to be fruitful if the servant is not primarily baptized in the spirit of a suffering compassion. We can never heal the wounds we do not feel. Tearless hearts can never be heralds of the passion. We must bleed if we would be ministers of the saving blood. "Put on, therefore, as God's elect, a heart of compassion."

--J. H. Jowett, D.D.

THE OLD TESTAMENT ILLUSTRATION

The word WIN used so frequently in connection with the theme of these studies may legitimately be applied to the captivating of human affections. The figure of the bridegroom wooing and winning his bride is elevated to the spiritual realm by the apostle Paul, who speaks of the believer as one who is married to another," even to Christ (Ro 7:4). No more beautiful illustration of the work of the soul-winner can be found in Holy Writ than the winning of Rebekah for Isaac by Eliezer, Abraham's servant. The delicate task entrusted to **ELIEZER-- THAT OF WINNING A BRIDE FOR ISAAC--**has a present-day parallel in the task of the Christian worker who seeks to win for Christ a bride. Let us study this servant and his methods as recounted in Genesis 24, first reading the chapter through.

I. HIS QUALIFICATIONS

1. He was born in Abraham's house (Gen 15:3), and thus had **AN INTIMATE KNOWLEDGE OF HIS MASTER, AND OF HIS PLANS** for Isaac, his only son. The soul-winner too must, through close and intimate fellowship with God, enter into His purposes for His only Son.

2. His whole life was unreservedly **YIELDED TO THE SERVICE OF THE ONE WHO SUPPLANTED HIM,** for Eliezer would have been heir to all Abraham's wealth had Isaac not been born (Gen 15:2-4; 24:36, with Jo 3:30).

II. HIS MISSION

1. **ABRAHAM REVEALED TO HIM HIS SECRET PURPOSE** to obtain a wife for his son, and God has similarly given us to know His secret purpose for His only begotten (Ac 15:14).

2. **ELIEZER RECEIVED DEFINITE INSTRUCTIONS** Where to go, and where not to go It was useless to go where the chosen bride was not. He was not bound to approach **EVERY** young woman he met. Therefore, the soul-winner is not called upon to speak to **EVERY** person who crosses his path, but only to those to whom he is directed by the Holy Spirit. Willingness to press the claims of Christ on anyone, anywhere, together with an attentive ear to the guidance of the Spirit, will

3. **HE WAS ROBBED OF ALL HONOR, BUT FREED OF ALL RESPONSIBILITY.** An angel was to precede him (Gen 15:7), who would prepare the heart of the chosen bride for the favorable reception of the message--a gracious ministry fulfilled for the soul-winner by the Holy Spirit. In the event of the woman being unwilling to accompany him after he had given the invitation, he was freed from all responsibility (Gen 15:8). Our responsibility extends only to the faithful delivery of God's message.

III. HIS ATTITUDE

1. **HE DID NOT UNDERESTIMATE THE DIFFICULTY** of persuading a woman to go with him, a stranger, to be the bride of one whom she had never seen. He knew the gain and glory of being a bride of Isaac, but she had no such knowledge. So the Christian worker knows the unsearchable riches of Christ; but as he has nothing to appeal to the senses of his "prospect," he sometimes fears that his Master will meet with rejection. It is just here that he must rely on the ministry of the angel.

2. **HE PROPOSED A CARNAL EXPEDIENT**--to take Isaac with him. Abraham indignantly rejected the proposal (Gen 15:6). Isaac had to be offered to the woman in a verbal message by the chosen

messenger. Sometimes the Word of God seems painfully inadequate to lure a soul away from the world to Christ. Yet, when this sword is wielded in the power of the Spirit, it is "quick and powerful." It is still true that "faith cometh by hearing, and hearing by the word of God."

3. **HIS DEPENDENCE ON THE ANGEL DID NOT CUT THE NERVE OF HIS OWN ENDEAVORS.** He prayed and acted as though all depended on him. He knew that God had chosen Isaac's bride, but he still prayed that he might be led to the one of God's choice, and put himself in the way of God's leading. He ventured forth in faith. "I, being in the way, the Lord led me." The pilot cannot guide the ship while it is moored to the wharf.

4. **HE SUBORDINATED HIS OWN COMFORT AND INTERESTS** to those of his master. He never obtruded himself. He speaks of "my master" (Gen 15:12,27,34). He would not so much as satisfy his hunger till he had unburdened his heart (Gen 15:33). The lesson is obvious.

IV. HIS METHOD

1. **HE PRAYED before he made the proposal** Gen 15:12), and during the negotiations (Gen 15:26), nor did he forget to praise God as he saw his prayers being answered (Gen 15:15).

2. **HE DELIVERED HIS MESSAGE CLEARLY AND SIMPLY.** Abraham had one wonderful son, on whom he had bestowed all his wealth. He desired a bride for his son, and Rebekah was the bride of divine choice. Would she consent? "The Father loveth the Son, and hath given all things into his hand." The worker's task is to present clearly and winsomely the facts of the Gospel, in order to induce souls to accept the Son.

3. **HE USED NO UNDUE PRESSURE,** although he was most anxious for the answer to be "Yes." He left that to the angel. There is always a thrilling pause when a soul is brought to the point of decision for Christ, but it is the work of the Spirit to draw that soul to say "Yes" to Christ. The wise worker will not force a decision. Eliezer even tarried a whole night to give her time to reflect on the offer. (Doubtless he spent most of it in prayer.) He was well rewarded for an anxious night when she responded: "I will go."

4. **HE EXPECTED SUDDEN SUCCESS.** Less than a day had elapsed before the bride was on her way to meet Isaac! However, she had opposition. Her mother and brother wanted her to stay at least ten months. Eliezer would not hear of it. "Hinder me not!" Satan is the prince of delays, but a soul is too precious to win and nearly lose again. Expect sudden conversions.

Our last glimpse of Eliezer is in communion with his Isaac (Gen 15:56). He has fulfilled his mission. He has brought the bride to the bridegroom. He gives an account of the way he had been prospered, and then fades out of the picture, leaving Isaac alone with Rebekah. When we are granted success in our mission, let us emulate his self-effacement.

Chapter 6

THE NEW TESTAMENT EXAMPLE

Has it ever occurred to you that the greater part of the harvest of our Lord's earthly ministry was hand-gathered fruit? Seven out of the eleven apostles, and probably the other four as well, were won by individual appeal. In both Matthew and John, at least **SIXTEEN PRIVATE INTERVIEWS** are recorded for our instruction. Surely, this is sufficient evidence that the Master considered personal soul winning as of primary importance. In this, as in everything else, He is our Exemplar.

Christ was THE MASTER SOUL-WINNER. Knowing, as He did, what was in man (Jo 2:25), and the workings of the human mind which He had fashioned, His methods in dealing with various classes will be of the greatest interest and importance to His followers. Let us learn some lessons from Him.

1. **HE WAS NOT CLASS-CONSCIOUS.** He had conversations with the ruling class, e.g., Nicodemus and the young ruler. He conversed with businesspersons, men of the middle class, e.g., Zaccheus. Nevertheless, He did not neglect to deal with the outcasts, e.g., the woman of Samaria. He gave of His very best to each class.

2. **HE MADE A TACTFUL APPROACH.** It was His frequent habit to commence with some point of common interest, from which He could lead the

conversation on to spiritual realities. His question to the leper was: "Wilt thou be made whole?"--a matter of burning interest. He met Nicodemus on the ground of his interest in the Kingdom of God. He led the conversation with the woman of Samaria from well water to living water. He told fisherman Peter that He would make him a fisher of men.

3. **HE COMMENDED RATHER THAN CONDEMNED.** Honest commendation is one of the quickest avenues of approach into the human heart. Our Lord doubtless perceived many defects in the character of Nathanael, but He opened the conversation by commending him on his freedom from guile. Probably nothing will more quickly dissipate prejudice than this approach. Condemnation always alienates and closes the heart against further advances.

4. **HE CONSTANTLY ILLUSTRATED** His talks with simple parables which were within the range of knowledge of His auditors. One of the evangelists said that "without a parable spake he not unto them."

5. **HE REFUSED TO BE DRAWN INTO PROFITLESS ARGUMENT.** When faced with an argumentative lawyer who demanded an answer to his quibbling question: "Who is my neighbor?" the Lord so completely disarmed him with the parable of the Good Samaritan, that he had no further

argument to present. He refused to be sidetracked from the main issue.

6. **HE WEPT AND PRAYED** over the souls of men, believing that unless He sowed in tears He would not reap in joy. He gladly inconvenienced Himself if He could only be a blessing to someone.

7. **HE NEVER FAILED TO MAKE A PERSONAL APPLICATION OF HIS TEACHINGS.** In inducing her friends to come to see Christ, the woman of Samaria said: "Come, see a man who told me all things that ever I did." To Nicodemus He said: "Ye must be born again."

8. **HIS BLAMELESS LIFE** constituted the power of His spoken testimony.

AN EXAMPLE

THE CASE--The Woman of Samaria (Jo 4)

(a) Adulteress

(b) Sensitive, not shameless This is seen in her going at noon, when no one in the East thinks of going for water.

(c) Religious formalist

(d) Proud of her descent (Jo 4:12)

(e) Frivolous (Jo 4:15) She had a tongue quick to turn grave things into jests.

THE METHOD

    (a)   He went out of His way.

    (b)   He was not bound by conventionality. "Let no one talk with a woman in the street; no, not with his own wife" (Rabbis).

    (c)   Acted circumspectly Did not arrange to meet her at dusk, but at noon.

    (d)   Put Himself to inconvenience to meet her.

    (e)   He was tactful.

- Did not interview her in the presence of others.
- Did not reproach or scold her.
- He asked a favor.
- Sought to teach spiritual truth through homely metaphor.
- After a while ceased to beat about the bush (Jo 4:16), getting into close quarters.
- He refused to be diverted (Jo 4:19,20).
- Yet He did not ignore the point she had raised (Jo 4:21).

It is interesting to notice further the barriers which the woman raised in self-defense. The sex barrier (Jo 4:9). The racial barrier (Jo 4:9). The religious barrier (Jo 4:19,20). But the Lord ruthlessly demolished them all, and exposed her heart to her own gaze. She tried in every way possible to avoid the issue, but Christ kept her to it. She appealed to her ancestry (Jo 4:12), told a half-truth in an endeavor to conceal her guilt (Jo 4:17), concurred in what He said and endeavored to flatter Him (Jo 4:17); but in each case He brought her back to her guilt and need.

The culmination of the interview is seen in verses Jo:4:25,26-- the revelation of Himself as the Messiah--the sole objective of all personal work.

When I am dying how glad I shall be That the lamp of my life has been blazed out for Thee. I shall be glad in whatever I gave, Labor, or money, one sinner to save; I shall not mind that the path has been rough, That Thy dear feet led the way is enough. When I am dying how glad I shall be, that the lamp of my life has been blazed out for Thee. **OPPORTUNITY, APPROACH, AND DIAGNOSIS**

I. **OPPORTUNITY**

> All our natural endowments, all our personal histories, all our contrasted circumstances, are so many opportunities for peculiar work.
>
> **--Bishop Wescott**

Although this theme has already been briefly mentioned in a previous study, it is deserving of more particular treatment.

In the studio of an ancient Greek sculptor stood a rather peculiar piece of work. It was a statue, the hair of whose head was thrown around to cover the face; on each foot there was a wing, and the statue was standing on its toes. The visitor asked for its name, and the sculptor said it was "Opportunity."

"Why is its face veiled?" he asked.

"Because men seldom know her when she comes to them," was the reply. "And why does she stand upon her toes, and why the wings?"

"Because," said the sculptor, "when once she is gone, she can never be overtaken."

A great Christian worker entered a store and 'something' said: "Speak to the clerk; speak to the clerk!" Instead of doing it he went out. However, the voice kept speaking for an hour, and at last he went back and asked for the clerk. The proprietor said: "We had an awful tragedy here a few minutes ago. Immediately after you went out the clerk that waited on you went into the back room and shot a bullet through his brain. He is back there now if you wish to see him."

Thus was opportunity irretrievably lost--and with what eternal consequences. Our path is bestrewn with opportunities, most of which are unseen or unembraced. "While thy servant was busy here and there, the man was gone."

1. **IN THE HOME** A friend, anxious to serve her Lord, saw in the man who came to blow out her gas meter a candidate for eternity, pressed on him the claims of Christ, and had the joy of leading him to her Lord. Another friend saw and seized a similar opportunity with the milkman who came weekly to collect her account, with a similar blessed result. Have you no such

opportunities? And what about your own children? Have you improved the numberless opportunities you have had of definitely leading them to the feet of the Savior? In # 2Ki 5:1-5 we are told how a housemaid brought salvation to the home of the Syrian General. Lord Shaftsbury was led to Christ through one of his housemaids. Andrew brought his own brother Peter to Christ. The home circle has a prior claim on our witness.

2. **IN THE SUNDAY SCHOOL OR BIBLE CLASS** It is not sufficient to put the way of salvation before the class in general. It is the teacher's privilege and duty to lovingly press the claims of Christ on the individual scholar, not in the presence of others, but perhaps at the teacher's home. What a joy it would be to win your whole class for Christ. One leader known to the writer recently began a Bible class for his schoolboys. Today thirty of them have been won for Christ.

3. **AT AFTERNOON TEA PARTIES** "I am not satisfied with our At Homes," said one lady to another. "We talk of our neighbors, the latest picture or book, but surely it is a great waste of time. Why should we not pray over our callers and then set to work to bring some better influence to bear on them." Next day, amid the rustle of silks and mingled odors of flowers, there somehow came to be felt a consciousness of God which made talking about Him perfectly natural. Nor was it surprising that one should have said: "We have

stayed an unconscionable time today, but one seldom gets a talk like this, and one hungers for it without knowing it." Few see such openings on social occasions.

4. **IN THE CHURCH** An invitation from the preacher for any who desire conversation on spiritual matters to meet him in the vestry, has been a fruitful method of soul winning. A wise and winsome inquiry as to how they enjoyed the service, by a member of the congregation, may reveal the fact that the stranger is anxious to converse on spiritual topics.

5. **IN TRAVEL** Buses, trains, and boats, will each provide the zealous soul-winner with opportunities of making his Master known. Sir George Williams, founder of the YMCA, when crossing the Atlantic, made a point of speaking to every soul on board from captain to stoker, from card-player in the smoking room to emigrant in the steerage, and the remarkable thing is that he could never recollect a single instance when he received a rude or mocking retort. The writer has had many remarkable experiences and evidence of God's leading in conversation with fellow travelers, or with others when waiting for trains.

D. L. Moody made it the practice of his life to speak to men on the streetcars. It is related of him that in thus dealing with a man on a Detroit streetcar, he asked him the question: "Are you a Christian?" The man answered: "No, sir, but I wish I were." Mr. Moody there and then led the man to Christ. We don't have many street cars today, we do have buses and trains.

    6.   **AMONG YOUR OWN CLASS** A soldier can most effectively reach a soldier, or a society woman one of her own class. An invalid would have a fine point of contact with another shut-in, and a nurse with a nurse.

Chapter 7

THE APPROACH

The soul-winner should covet and cultivate an easy manner of approach to religious subjects, for it requires tact and skill to turn the conversation from secular to sacred subjects. He must be always ready to converse about Christ, and a few suggestions as to how best to do this follow.

Be natural in manner and in tone of voice. Let it be seen that your religion forms a joyous part of your everyday life. Some onlookers at an open-air service a few days ago remarked: "They don't seem to get very much kick out of it." Let us show by our manner that we enjoy Christ.

Study the art of diverting conversation to spiritual topics as did Jesus with the woman of Samaria. A student was taking a photograph of the "LURLINE" as she lay alongside the wharf. A youth standing near volunteered the statement, "I suppose she's as safe as Hell." The student immediately asked him if he considered Hell safe, diverted the conversation into spiritual channels, and led him to Christ.

A man was endeavoring to sell a stain-remover to a Christian housewife. After buying it (an important element in the approach), she said: "I know something which will remove stains too." "What is that?" he inquired. The door was now open and she replied, "The blood of Jesus Christ."

Let's Go Soul Winning

Have something to offer, whether it be a tract, an invitation to a service, or a Gospel. Supposing the tract was "God's Way of Salvation," the person could be approached thus: "Would you mind accepting a little booklet to read?" spoken with a cheery smile. "It tells God's way of salvation. Do you know God's way of salvation?" "I'm not sure if I do." "Would you mind if I told you?" If the tract were "The Reason Why," the orker could say: "This little booklet tells the reason why no one can afford to be without Christ. I wonder if you know Christ as your personal Savior. Do you?" In this way it is easy to enter on a conversation which may lead to the salvation of a soul.

It is often helpful to put the person under some obligation to you, such as by lending your newspaper on the train, or doing some other little service which will create a spirit of comradeship.

Sometimes the direct question, "Are you a Christian?" leads to a successful conversation. This was the usual method adopted by Uncle John Vassar, a wonderful soul-winner who was a member of Dr. A. J. Gordon's church in Boston. On one occasion he addressed this question to two ladies. "Certainly," they replied.

"Have you been born again?" he asked.

"This is Boston," said the ladies, "and you know we don't believe in that doctrine here."

He immediately produced his Bible and showed what God has to say on the subject. In a short time they were on their knees. That evening one of the ladies told her husband of her encounter with Uncle John Vassar.

"I wish I had been there," said the man.

"What would you have done?" asked his wife.

"I would have told him to go about his business."

"But if you had been there, you would have said he WAS about his business."

THE DIAGNOSIS

The first task of the physician is correctly to diagnose the case, or his prescription will be at random. So with the soul-physician. The doctor asks questions so couched as to reveal the inward condition, and the doctor of souls must do the same. The questions at first may be general, but must proceed to the particular. Is he a backslider, a non-witnessing Christian, ignorant of the simple plan of salvation, ensnared by some cult, clinging to some sin, skeptical, or hindered by some honest difficulties? This can be found out only by careful questioning. Commence by saying: "Have you ever made a decision for Christ?" If the answer is in the affirmative, next ascertain whether he was really born again. If the answer is again in the affirmative, inquire what has led to his present unsatisfactory condition. But if, on the other hand, it has been merely a "decision," deal as though the person was unconverted, and lead him to Christ. In subsequent chapters, instruction will be given as to how to deal with those who have been ensnared by cults, have honest difficulties, or make dishonest excuses.

The following story related by Howard W. Pope shows the importance of correct diagnosis. Let me give it in his words. "I was asked to speak to a certain man in an inquiry meeting in Northfield. Before I reached him, another worker began to talk to him, and I turned to others. Later I saw the other worker leaving him, and approaching him I said: 'Have you settled the great question?' 'No,' said the other worker, 'he is going away unsaved because he will not give his heart to God.' 'What is the trouble?' I inquired. I soon surmised that it was not a case of stubborn unwillingness to yield to Christ, but rather a lack of confidence in his ability to make the surrender real. I told him that if he would surrender, Christ would enable him to make the surrender good. I then suggested that we kneel, and that he follow me sentence by sentence while I led in prayer. He said he did not know whether he could honestly do it. 'Follow me as far as you can and then stop,' I replied. He consented, and we knelt down together and I led him in a committal to Christ as strong and complete as I knew how to make it, going cautiously, of course, at first, but making it stronger as I saw his willingness to follow. When we arose, he told the first person he met that he had accepted Christ as his Savior." The first worker failed because he had made a false diagnosis, mistaking the man's lack of confidence for stubborn willfulness.

The diagnosis, of course, must be followed by the prescribing of the appropriate remedy, which subject will engage us in the next chapter. We now turn to the actual work of dealing with both the professedly converted and the unconverted. Let us first think of the former class.

Chapter 8

CONVERTED PERSONS.

Those with whom you will come in contact, who need personal dealing, may be divided into two main classes: those who are open backsliders, and those whose Christian experience is unsatisfactory.

1. **OPEN BACKSLIDERS.** It is assumed that you have made sure that the person with whom you are dealing was genuinely converted, and are satisfied as to whether he is a possessor or merely a professor.

    If the person **DOES NOT SEEM ANXIOUS TO RETURN** to the Lord, and shows no real sorrow, although at times he longs for "the good old days," use Je 2:5,13,17,19, showing the ingratitude, bitterness, and folly of his longer pursuing his godless way. Bring him face to face with the inevitable issues of his conduct in the life to come. Use also 1Ki 11:9 Am 4:11 Lu 11:24 2Pe 2:20-22.

    If, however, the person manifests a **GENUINE SORROW FOR SIN AND DESIRE TO RETURN** to the Lord, it is a great joy to bring the healing balm of the Scriptures to his sad heart. Note how gently the Lord dealt with penitent Peter: "Go and tell my disciples AND PETER." Let us, too, be gentle in our dealing.

Our first task is to assure him of God's willingness to receive all who return to Him. Use Ho 14:1-4 with its joyous promise of restoration. Lu 15:11-24 has been wonderfully used in encouraging wanderers to return from the far country.

NEXT get him down on his knees and compel a full and unvarnished confession and forsaking of sin (Jer 3:13; 1Jo 1:9). This is absolutely essential to restoration.

Then show that if he has done his part--confessing, acknowledging, and forsaking his sin--God has done His part, forgiving, cleansing, and restoring. Get him to thank God for having received him back into His fellowship. In some cases it may induce brokenness to go through Ps 51:1 with the inquirer.

2. **THOSE THAT CHRISTIAN EXPERIENCE HAS BEEN UNSATISFACTORY** first ascertain the reason. The causes of spiritual decline are much the same in most cases: neglect of prayer, Bible reading, or witnessing, worldliness, indulgence of sin or doubt, no assurance of salvation, no victory over sin.

(a) **NEGLECT OF PRAYER**--a sadly common neglect among Christians, and probably, along with neglect of the Bible, the most fruitful cause of backsliding. Some time ago the writer met a fine young man, truly converted and anxious to go on for God, and yet who was making no progress. In response to a question he admitted that he did not regularly read and pray. On having the part which prayer and Bible reading play in the

Christian life explained to him, he said: "I did not know, and no one ever told me that this was necessary to growth in the Christian life." It was touching to hear him pray as though God had given him a great revelation. Never take it for granted that the young convert will automatically read and pray. Instruct him on this point. Endeavor to find the reason for the lack of prayer and suggest possible causes (Ja 4:2). Show the value of a quiet time (Mt 6:6). Quote Christ's example (Mt 14:13,23 Mr 1:35), as well as that of other saints (Ps 55:17 Da 6:10 Mt 26:41 Ep 6:18).

(b) **NEGLECT OF THE BIBLE** Show the place the Bible must ever hold in the life of the happy Christian. Ask why it is that it seems so difficult to find time for Bible reading and prayer, and yet time is found for everything else. Suggest that the reason is that the Devil knows if he can prevent this he will paralyze the whole of the believer's life of service. Use 1Pe 2:2 Ja 1:21,22; #2Ti 3:15-17; a passage which shows the part the Bible plays in saving from error and equipping for service; Ps 119:9,130, one of the secrets of victory; Ps 1:1,2 Jo 5:38,39 Ac 17:11 Jo 8:31.

(c) **NEGLECT IN WITNESSING.** In many cases the real joy of salvation is never experienced until open confession has been made. Ascertain if the inquirer has ever done this, and if he is still witnessing. If not, show that this is the cause of the unsatisfactory experience. One who is ashamed of Jesus cannot be happy. Use Ro 10:9,10; Mt 10:32,33. Witnessing is part of the believer's duty as well as his privilege. If the reason of non-witness is fear of ridicule or persecution, use Jo-12:42,43. Encourage personal work with Dan 12:3 Pr 11:30; Php 4:13.

(d) **COMPROMISE WITH THE WORLD**

Since Ja 4:4 is true and "friendship with the world is enmity with God," it naturally follows that the Christian who is on good terms with the world is not on good terms with God, and VICE VERSA. God has commanded us to be separate from the world and not to love it (1 Jo 2:15-17 2Co 6:14-7:1 Mt 6:24 Lu 8:14). Bring the inquirer to the point where he will make a definite and final break with the world (1Co 6:19,20 8:13 Col.3:17 1Tim 4:6 1Co 6:12).

(e) **ENSLAVED BY SIN** A man in one of Moody's meetings said he would like to come, but he was chained and couldn't come. A Scotsman said to him: "Aye, man, why don't you come, chain and all?" He said: "I never thought of that." The One who saved from the guilt of sin is able to save from its enslaving power (Ro 6:11; 1Co 15:57).

(f) **NO ASSURANCE OF SALVATION**

The cause of this may ge ignorance. Many have no idea that a believer can, before he dies, know with certainty that he is saved. With this class of person, use 1Jo 5:10-13, stressing the last verse. Also Jo 1:12 3:36 5:24; and Ac 13:39. Make clear what believing on Christ really means, and make sure that this saving belief is present.

Sometimes, however, the lack of assurance is due to tolerated sin. In such a case, find out what is hindering, press for a confession, and assurance will generally result. Use Is 55:7 Jo 8:12 Ps 32:1-5.

A very general cause of lack of assurance is a dependence on feeling. Sometimes the inquirer feels saved, but at other times he is sure he is not saved. The task of the worker is to induce him to cease from looking at his own inward feelings and to rest on the sure Word of God. Tell him that God's unchanging Word is far more trustworthy than his fickle feelings. Use such a verse as Jo 3:36, calling attention to the fact that "believing" is assuredly followed by "having" eternal life. Ro 8:1 and Jo 5:24 assure that for the believer judgment is past. Eternal life is given, and cannot be taken away. Jo 10:28,29 Ex 12:1-13 have been much used in this connection. The sprinkled blood ensured safety while the Word of the Lord believed assured of safety. An old lady, full of joyous confidence, was asked: "But suppose Christ should let you slip through His fingers?" She replied at once: "But I AM one of His fingers." There is no possibility of the true believer being separated from the love of Christ (Ro 8:38,39). Do not let the inquirer go until he can say with absolute assurance: "I know that I have eternal life."

Chapter 9

UNCONVERTED PERSONS

These may be considered under five headings:

1. **ANXIOUS OR INTERESTED.** What a joy it is to the zealous personal worker to come across someone anxious to be saved. Some time ago a man came to my door of weeping so much that a minute elapsed before he could tell us his errand. "Have you a Bible here?" he inquired. "Certainly. Come in. What is troubling you? Do you know the joy of having your sins forgiven?" "No, but that's what I've come about." What a joy it was to lead this man to Christ, to see the cloud lift from his face, and to see his handkerchief, already saturated with tears of repentance, doing service again, but this time for tears of joy. The man, who lived hundreds of miles away, had been under conviction of sin for six months as a result of reading literature sent out from our ministry, and had made his way to us to find Christ. Unfortunately, such cases are all too rare. There seem to be very few who are really concerned and anxious about their souls.

The first thing to do with one in this condition is to assure him of God's willingness and ability to save (Lu 19:10). Next show that God requires repentance, or a sorrow for sin real enough to make him willing to forsake it (Ac 17:30 Lu 13:3 Is 55:7). Repentance involves confession, for God cannot forgive sin until it is confessed to Him (1 Jo 1:9). Then show what Christ had to suffer before God's love could have full sway, and He could righteously forgive men. It is often very effective to have the seeker read Is 53:3-6, using the first person singular instead of plural, e.g., "Surely he hath borne by grief's. ... He was wounded for my transgressions and bruised for my iniquities," etc. This will accomplish the dual purpose of convicting of sin and awakening faith in Christ. Endeavor to make the picture as graphic as possible. Having got the inquirer to repent and confess his need, and explained the cost at which the gift of eternal life was bought, the next step is to show that before he can be saved he must not only repent but believe the Gospel (Mr 1:15 Ac 16:31). Nevertheless, what is it to believe?

WHAT IT IS TO BELIEVE

It is of the utmost importance that the personal worker is able to show clearly the nature of saving faith, or what is meant in Scripture by "believe on the Lord Jesus Christ." The sin for which men are condemned is--" Because they believe not on me" (Jo 16:9).

In a letter received recently, an inquirer said, "I believe in Christ, but the devils also believe and tremble, and they are not saved." Here is the worker's problem concisely. There are obviously two kinds of belief--one purely mental, the other involving the whole of the moral nature. The purely mental opinion that it is true that Christ lived and died for men, works no saving change in the heart or life. What, then, is it to believe to the salvation of your soul? It is so to put your confidence in Christ as being what He claimed to be--your Savior and Sin-bearer--that you put yourself absolutely in His hands for salvation. If I am suffering from a dread disease for which a certain surgeon says he has an unfailing remedy, it is not sufficient that I believe that he can cure me. That is merely an opinion. I do not really believe until I put my case in his hands. I do not believe in my banker until I place my money in his keeping. Believing without trusting is not faith. Perhaps no illustration is more effective than that of Blondin, the tight-rope walker who, having walked the tight-rope across Niagara Falls, first alone, and then pushing a wheelbarrow, asked a little fellow who had been watching him breathlessly, whether he believed that he could wheel him across the rope in the barrow. "Of course I do, sir," replied the lad, "I saw you do it." "All right, jump in." "Oh, no, sir, you don't catch me," was the honest reply. He believed (mentally), but he did not trust.

Another way of presenting this truth is by showing from John 1:12 that believing and receiving are synonymous. "As many as received him"--as personal Savior and Sin-bearer--thereby received "power to become the sons of God."

The final step is to lead the inquirer definitely to believe in Christ and receive Him as Savior. Use Jo 1:11,12 again, somewhat as follows: "You have now confessed your sin and need. You believe that when Jesus died He bore the punishment for your sins and that He longs to be your Savior and Master. Will you now take Him to be such?" "Yes, I will." "Well, what does this verse say you are now?" **"A child of God."** "And you are really a child of God already?" If the inquirer is not clear on this point, go over the ground again. Do not leave him until the last doubt has been removed.

Another verse, which I frequently use, is Jo 5:24: "Have you heard God's Word about Christ tonight?" "Yes." "Well, what does God say you have?" **"Everlasting life."** "And have you everlasting life?" If hesitancy is shown, take him back over the ground until he can give an unequivocal "Yes." "And will you ever be brought into judgment for your sins?" **"No."** "Why not," "Because Jesus bore the judgment for me." The worker may have to supply this answer. "And what other change has taken place?" "I have passed from death unto life." "Then let us get down on our knees and thank Him for His gift."

It is well to emphasize the divine order--the fact, faith, and then feeling.

Jesus did it--on the cross.

God says it--in His Word.

I believe it--in my heart.

Feeling that you are saved cannot come before you ARE saved, any more than feeling you are well after an illness can come before you are well as you cannot be saved without believing, faith must precede feeling. As faith must have a fact to rest on, the fact must precede faith. Many inquirers want to feel saved before they believe in Christ, and they make their feelings the test as to whether or not they have believed, thus reversing the divine order. I believe it, not because I feel it, but because God says it and Jesus did it. Make sure that the anxious one is not resting in his own feelings but on God's Word.

Go and find them ere they perish, Tell them of the Savior's love;
How He came to guide them safely To the Father's home above.
Go and find them in their darkness, Bound by chains of slavery;
Tell abroad the proclamation; Jesus Christ can set them free.
Go and find them, hasten! Hasten! Time is fleeting fast away;
They are dying, lost and hopeless while you linger day by day.

Chapter 10

THE INDIFFERENT OR CARELESS

Many circumstances have combined to cause this group to preponderate between the unsaved--wrong doctrine in the pulpits, worldliness in the church, changing conditions in the world, the decay of home life and family religion, Sunday desecration, and the growing number of cults. Accordingly, the worker must know how to arouse these unconcerned ones from their indifference.

(a) **PRODUCE CONVICTION OF SIN.**
This is accomplished not by argument or persuasion, but by presenting appropriate Scriptures, relying on the Holy Spirit to apply them and "convict of sin, righteousness and judgment." Dr. Torrey shows how to use effectively Ro 14:12 in this connection. "First get your prospect to read it and ask him: 'Who has to give account?' **'Every one of us,'** 'who does that take in?' **'Me,'** 'who, then, is to give account?' 'I am.' 'To whom are you to give account?' 'To God' 'Of what are you to give account?' 'Of myself' 'Read it that way.' 'I shall give an account of myself unto God.' 'Are you ready to do it?'" By this time, indifference will be turning into concern. Show that he has only to continue as he is, neglecting God's salvation, to be lost (Heb. 2:3).

Other Scriptures are 1Jo 3:14 Rev 21:8; Ro 3:22, 23 Mr 7:21-23 Ro 8:7; Gal 3:10. Mt 22:36-38 Ja 2:10 are effective in showing the greatness of sin; Ro 6:23 Jo 3:36 8:34 in showing the consequences of sin. Jo 3:17-19 reveal that unbelief in Christ is an appalling and damning sin, while Heb 10:28-29 warns of the awful punishment of those who despise the blood of Christ.

(b) **POINT TO CHRIST THE CRUCIFIED.** Having been satisfied that there has been real conviction of sin, point out the way of salvation. Another method is to use the ABC of salvation. "All have sinned" (Ro3:23). "Behold the Lamb of God" (Jo 1:29). "Come unto me" (Mt 11:28). Press home the love God has for sinners (Is 53:5,6 Jo 3:16 1Pe 2:24).

THOSE WHO HAVE RAISED OBJECTIONS OR HAVE DIFFICULTIES

These difficulties: may be grouped under four headings

- Relating to the Bible or its doctrines
- Based on the inconsistencies of Christians
- Personal difficulties
- Arising from teaching of Cults

(a) OBJECTIONS RELATING TO THE BIBLE OR ITS DOCTRINES

"THE BIBLE IS FULL OF CONTRADICTIONS." Hand your Bible over to the objector and ask him to show you one or two. Do not accept a verbal statement; make him show them to you from the Bible. This he will almost certainly be unable to do. The bladder once pricked, the way will be open for you to call attention to fulfilled prophecies, the marvelous structural and organic unity of the Book, the confirmations of archaeology, etc. Then, turning to 1Co 2:14, tell him that the reason he cannot understand the Bible is that he is a faculty short and needs to be born again as commanded in Jo 3:3,7, and after which he would be able to understand the Scriptures.

"THE BIBLE IS IMPURE." This is indeed a strange objection, seeing that the holiest and purest minds in all ages have found their greatest joy in the Scriptures. Use Tit 1:15 2Pe 2:11,12. Contrast with the psalmist, who said: "Thy word is very pure: therefore thy servant loveth it" (Ps 119:140). The accounts in the Bible of the wickedness of men and women are the faithful charting of sunken rocks for the admonition of voyagers on the ocean of life. The Bible depicts life as it is, and shows the awful consequences of sin both in this life and in that to come.

"NO SUCH BEING AS GOD EXISTS." The Bible nowhere undertakes to prove the existence of God, but everywhere takes it for granted. Gen 1:1 asserts His eternity. We are surrounded with evidence of His existence, which must be indisputable to any but one blinded with prejudice. The existence of a watch predicates the existence of a watchmaker. The sound of harmonious music argues for the existence of a musician. The existence of a harmoniously running universe, vast in magnitude yet perfect in detail, argues the existence of an infinitely wise and powerful God (Ro 1:19-23 Ps 8:1,3 33:6). This God is fully revealed in Christ (2Co 4:6).

"THERE IS NO SUCH PLACE AS HELL." True, the doctrine of eternal punishment is growing more and more unpopular, but it is nonetheless true. The denier of this doctrine plays on the words **DEATH, DESTRUCTION, EVERLASTING, ETERNAL**. He can give you, he says the meaning of the words from the original, but his object is to prove his view, not to expound God's view. Read such Scriptures as Jo 3:36 Mt 25:46 Rev 20:10,15 21:8 Mr 9:43,44 to anyone with an unprejudiced mind, and he will undoubtedly say that, little as he likes the thought, these Scriptures unite to teach a future Hell and everlasting punishment for the finally impenitent. The same Hell as is to be occupied by the Devil and his underlings is to be the final abode of the wicked. In Lu 16:26, whatever else Christ meant to teach, at least He taught that there was an eternally fixed gulf between Lazarus and the rich man. The expressions **AGES OF AGES, or FOREVER AND EVER**, in their only reasonable interpretation mean "eternal." Nowhere does Christ suggest any limitation of time for either reward or suffering, nor does He suggest any termination of the doom of the lost. This is an awful truth, and must be tenderly presented, but it should prove a strong incentive to the soul-winner to "go for souls."

"GOD IS TOO LOVING TO CONDEMN ANYONE." Ask him from what source he derived his conception of the character of God. Was it not from the Bible? Well, if he believed the Bible in its assurance of God's love, he must be consistent and accept also its warning of God's wrath, for it reveals God as not only loving but just (2Pe 3:9). Get the objector to compare 1 Jo 4:8 with Heb 12:29. Although God is loving and good, man must beware of abusing God's goodness (Ro 2:4,5). The purpose of God's goodness is to lead men to repentance. In 2Pe 2:4-6 it is clearly revealed that God's love did not prevent His justice being exercised and His judgment falling on the wicked antediluvians.

"THE BIBLE IS NOT INSPIRED." First, ask the objector what he means by "inspired." In nine cases out of ten, the argument ends when you press him to define his terms. Strong defines inspiration thus: "The special divine influence upon the minds of the Scripture writers in view of which their productions, apart from errors of transcription, and when rightly interpreted, constitute the infallible rule of faith and practice." Then state that his disbelief does not affect the fact at all (Ro3:3,4). The following Scriptures may be used in proving their inspiration: 2Ti 3:15,16 1The 2:13 2Pe 1:19-21 Heb 4:12. Usually one who quibbles on this point has read more about the Scriptures than he has of the Scriptures themselves, and a question as to whether he has ever read the Bible through from Genesis to Revelation would discomfit him. If he has never done that, he is hardly in a position to judge.

OBJECTIONS BASED ON THE INCONSISTENCIES OF CHRISTIANS.

"THERE ARE TOO MANY HYPOCRITES IN THE CHURCH." The worker will have to sadly admit that this is true in a measure, but it must be borne in mind that this is always an **EXCUSE, not a REASON,** for not accepting Christ, and therefore the person who advances it is himself a hypocrite, for he is not true to his convictions. Use Ro 14:12 Mt 7:1-5. Again, show if there are false Christians, there must be some who are real. I do not throw out of my pocket all my coins because there happens to be a counterfeit coin among them. Even if some Christians are frauds and hypocrites, Christ is no fraud, and it is to Him you are inviting sinners. The objector does not have to answer for the hypocrite but for himself. (Ro 14:12 Jo 21:21,22.) If he knows how Christians ought to live, let him set the example, for light brings corresponding responsibility (Lu 12:47).

If he does not like hypocrites on earth, tell him to beware lest he spend all eternity with them, for all hypocrites are outside the pearly gates.

"I HAVE BEEN TREATED WRONGLY BY CHRISTIANS." A man once said to his pastor that the reason he would not accept Christ was his partner, a professing Christian, once had wronged him. "That is your real reason?" Asked the minister, "It is." "Suppose we put it down in writing," said the minister, and drawing out his notebook, wrote: "The reason why I am not a Christian is that my partner, who claimed to be a Christian, robbed me in a business deal." Tearing out the leaf, he handed it to the man, saying, "When you come before the Great White Throne, and God asks you why you have rejected His Son, just hand him that paper," and turning away, he left him. Hardly had he reached home before the doorbell rang, and there stood the man with the paper in his hand. "I have brought this paper back," he said. "I am afraid it would not answer as an excuse to give to God." It was not long before that man was rejoicing in Christ. Even if a man has been wronged, that is no reason why he should do a still greater wrong to himself (Jo 3:36 2Th 1:7-9).

Chapter 11

PERSONAL DIFFICULTIES

"I AM NOT VERY BAD." That may be true according to one's own standard, but does he come up to God's standard? (Ro 3:10,23). Press these Scriptures home, showing that whatever he may be in his own eyes, he is a great sinner in God's sight, and show what sin really is. In any case, he admits that he is a sinner, and it is the fact of sin, not the quantity of sin, which is in question. A chain holding a ship does not need to be broken in every link to set the ship adrift; one link is enough (Ja 2:10). And the greatest sin of all is not believing on Christ (Jo 16:9).

"I AM DOING MY BEST." This is an old chestnut, but is still constantly produced But the best man's best is a failure in God's sight (Is 64:6). If our own works are to form the ground of our acceptance with God, then we must be flawless, perfect, whether in thought, word, or deed--which is impossible. "By the works of the law"--or by doing his best--" shall no flesh be justified" (Ga 2:16).

"I GO TO CHURCH." OR "I HAVE BEEN CONFIRMED." Many think that this constitutes the whole of man's duty to God, and take it for granted that when the time comes, they will be all right. Show that these things, though all right in the right place, do NOT take the place of the new birth (Jo 3:3,7). An alien who donned the American uniform without enlisting in the army would be looked upon as a spy, and shot. No one has a right to wear it unless he is a loyal soldier. Every converted person, and only such, should be connected in church fellowship with some body sound in the faith, but the mere joining of a church works no saving change.

"I HAVE ALWAYS BELIEVED IN CHRIST." A man will make this statement, when what he really means is that he believes some facts ABOUT Christ. Ask him "Then are you saved?" Usually the answer will be a direct negative, or at least a hesitating consent, and the way will be open, either to tell him how to be saved, or to explain what believing in Christ means.

"I CANNOT BELIEVE." In most cases, this is a question of morals, not of faith. Ask what sin he has in his life which is hindering belief, and the bow drawn at a venture will frequently be effective in striking at the hindering thing. Use Is 55:7. God says he CAN believe (Jo 1:12), and MUST believe (He 11:6). God never commands man to do what he is unable to do. Remove the hindrance and belief will be easy. Not to believe means judgment (Jo 3:18). Another effective method is to ask "Cannot believe whom? Can you not believe God?" "Yes, but I cannot believe myself." "You are not asked to. You must believe in Christ" (Ac 16:31; Jo 3:16).

"I HAVE TRIED BEFORE AND FAILED." The objector has evidently made the Christian life one of self-effort and this is at the root of his failure. Salvation does not come as a result of "trying," but of "trusting." Endeavor to find out the cause of failure by asking leading questions. "Did you trust in the finished work of Christ alone?" "Did you confess the Lord before men?" (Ro 10:9,10). In the majority of cases, the answer to this question will be "No," and you have discovered the cause of the failure. "Did you surrender absolutely to God?" (Ac 5:32). "Did you read the Bible and pray daily?" (1Pe 2:2 1Th 5:17). "Did you trust yourself or Christ to keep you from falling?" (2Co 12:9). "Have you done any work for Christ?" If your questioning satisfies you that the person was never truly converted, tell him that you can show him how not to fail. If he is converted, show him the excellent way. Jo 6:37 is applicable to both cases.

"I AM TOO WEAK." The remedy for such a person is to direct his attention away from himself to the Lord Christ. "It is not a question of your weakness, but of His strength" (Heb.7:25). Show God's willingness to help the weakest (2Co 9:10 Is 40:29-30). No one is too weak to trust the strong Christ. The keeping is not ours, but His (Jude 1:24 1Pe 1:5 2ti 1:12 Jo 10:28,29). There will be temptations, but also a way of escape (1Co 10:13). When God begins a work He finishes it (Php 1:6).

"I WILL WAIT TILL I AM BETTER." Many a man feels that he cannot come to Christ as he is, so he tries to improve himself by discontinuing some forms of sin and thus making himself worthy of God's salvation as though he could add anything to the perfect and finished work of Christ! Show that he is to come to Christ as he is, in all his sin and he will be received (Is 64:6 Lu 19:10 Mt 9:12,13); the parable of the Prodigal Son may be used as an illustration (Lu 15:18-24).

"I AM TOO BAD." Agree with the truth of this statement, rather than try to minimize his sinfulness. Tell him that if he could see as God sees, he would realize that he was a great deal more sinful than he thought. But Christ came to save bad sinners (Lu 19:10). In 1Ti 1:15, Paul claims that Christ saved the chief of sinners, so there is hope for all others (Isa 1:18 1Jo 1:7 Heb 7:25).

"I'VE DONE NO ONE ANY HARM." This is a very poor thing to boast about it would reflect little credit on him if he had done anyone any harm. Is that his main object in life? God requires not merely negative harmlessness, but positive holiness. Ask if he has come up to God's standard of holiness (Ro 3:23). Use also Mt 5:20.

"I SEE NO HARM IN INNOCENT PLEASURES OF THE WORLD." If friendship with the world is enmity with God, and the friend of the world is the enemy of God (Ja 4:4), then either God or the objector is wrong. The pleasures of the world are NOT innocent; there is a concealed hook in them all. Quote the example of Moses (He 11:24,25), but make abundantly clear the pleasure, pure and unalloyed, which results from union with Christ. A word of testimony to this effect might be helpful. Do not present this truth in a merely cold and negative fashion.

"THERE IS TOO MUCH TO GIVE UP." Even if it were necessary to give up everything, far better that than he should lose his soul (Mr 8:36). But God requires him to give up only that which is sinful and will therefore harm him. Quote Ps 84:11, **Psalm 84:11 (KJV)** ^{11} For the LORD God *is* a sun and shield: the LORD will give grace and glory: no good *thing* will he withhold from them that walk uprightly and testify on this point. Use **Romans 8:32 (KJV)** ^{32} He that spared not his own Son, but delivered him up for us all, how shall he not with him also freely give us all things?

"I CAN'T GIVE UP MY SINS." Show him that he will be lost unless he does (Ro 6:23 Gal 6:7,8 Rev 21:8). Do not compromise with the person as to the absolute necessity of his forsaking his sin, but show that he can forsake sin through the strength of Christ (Php 4:13), who when He receives him, will make him a new creature, no longer loving sin (Jo 8:36 1Jo 3:6-9); further show how to get victory over sin (Ro 6:12-14).

"I AM NOT YET READY TO COME." Most people intend to become Christians, but the Devil deludes them into postponing their acceptance of Christ. The following printed story impressed me: "A minister determined to preach on 'Now is the accepted time, now is the day of salvation.' While in his study thinking, he fell asleep and dreamed: he was carried into Hell and set down in the midst of a conclave of lost spirits they were assembled to devise means whereby they might damn the souls of men. One rose and said, 'I will go to earth and tell men the Bible is a fable.' No, that would not do. Another said, 'Let me go. I will tell men that there is no God, no Savior, no Heaven, and no Hell.' 'No, that will not do, we cannot make them believe THAT.' Suddenly one arose and with a wise mien suggested: 'I will tell men there is a God, a Savior, a Heaven, yes, and a Hell, too--but I will tell them there is no hurry; tomorrow will do, it will be even as today.' And they sent him." It would almost seem as though this was the Devil's trump card. Show this objector God's command (Ac 17:30); God's time (2Co 6:2). Urge the uncertainty of life (Pr 27:1 Ja 4:13-17). An unusual method is to show that God's time is now. Get the inquirer to tell you that God's time is now. Then take out your watch and say: "It is three o'clock now. Are you willing to accept Christ at three o'clock?" It is well to point out that God will not always be at the seeker's disposal. Use **Isaiah 55:6 (KJV)** ⁶ Seek ye the LORD while he may be found, call ye upon him while he is near: emphasizing "while." (Pr 29:1 Lu 12:19,20 Mt 24:44 Jo 7:33,34.)

"I WANT TO BE A CHRISTIAN, BUT I DON'T KNOW WHAT TO DO." It will be a joy to lead this individual to the Savior along the well-known road. First step, Repent (Ps 51:3,4). Second step, Believe (Acts 16:31 Jo 1:12). Third step, Confess (Ro10:9,10 Mt 10:32,33).

"I HAVE SOUGHT CHRIST, BUT HAVE NOT FOUND HIM." That certainly cannot be His fault, for He has said: "Ye shall seek me and find me when ye shall search for me with all your heart" (Jer 29:13). The trouble with this objector is insincerity, and not seeking with his whole heart.

"I AM AFRAID OF PERSECUTION." Show that the list of those cast into the lake of fire includes the fearful (Re 21:8). The Lord answered this objection in (Lu 12:4,5). (See also Pr 29:25 Is

51:7,8.) The early Christians had such joy in Christ that they rejoiced in suffering persecution for His sake (Ac 5:41). Think of the reward at the end (2Ti 2:12 Ro 8:18).

"I GUESS I'LL GET TO HEAVEN ALL RIGHT." He will if he is washed from his sins, but not unless (1Co 6:9,10 Re 21:27). He cannot come except through Christ, the only Way (Jo 14:6 1Ti 2:5 Ac 4:12).

"I WILL LOSE MY FRIENDS." It could be pointed out that if they are not friends of whom God could approve, he would be far better without them. (Ps 1:1,2). God here promises special blessing on one who renounces worldly friendships for His sake. In place of these godless friends, God will give first, His own friendship (1Jo 1:3), and then that of fellow Christians whose friendship is better than that of any godless man or woman (Mr 10:29,30).

"THE CHRISTIAN LIFE IS TOO HARD." Therefore, the Devil would have them believe. But the truth is that "the way of transgressors is hard" (Pr 13:15 Is 14:3), while Christ's yoke is easy and His burden light (Mt 11; 30). God's commands are NOT grevious (1Jo 5:3). The Christian life as depicted in (1Pe 1:8 does not seem so forbidding and exacting. It is true that the Christian life is one of discipline and involves enduring hardness, but there are such wonderful compensations that the true Christian counts these all joy (Ja 1:2).

"I HAVE NO FEELING." Remind the person that he is saved, not by feeling, but by believing (Jo 3:16 5:24 Ac 16:31); it is taking, receiving rather than feeling (Jo 1:12 Ro 6:23). Ask him if he can tell you of one Scripture where it says he must feel that he is saved before he can be saved. Let him believe first and he will have feeling enough after.

"I HAVE COMMITTED THE UNPARDONABLE SIN." First, be sure yourself as to the nature of the unpardonable sin. **Matthew 12:31-32 (KJV)** [31] Wherefore I say unto you, All manner of sin and blasphemy shall be forgiven unto men: but the blasphemy *against* the *Holy* Ghost shall not be forgiven unto men. [32] And whosoever speaketh a word against the Son of man, it shall be forgiven him: but whosoever speaketh against the Holy Ghost, it shall not be forgiven him, neither in this world, neither in the *world* to come. Read this in its context, where it is plain that this sin consists in deliberately attributing to the Devil the work which is known to have been wrought by the Holy Spirit. Ask the inquirer if he has done this. It is evident that one who is anxious about his soul cannot have committed this sin, since that anxiety is the direct result of the work of the Holy Spirit. Having shown what the sin is, hold the inquirer to Jo 6:37, with its unconditional promise that anyone, however good or bad, who comes to Christ, will in no wise be cast out. Do not give up until he "comes" to Christ.

Chapter 12

WORKING AMONG FALSE CULTS

ROMAN CATHOLICISM

The wise worker will remember that Roman Catholics have from childhood learned to revere their church, and resent any criticism of it. Any controversial issue should, therefore be avoided as far as possible. There are many things are held in common by both Catholic and Protestant, and these should be known by the worker, the deity of Christ, the atoning blood, the inspiration of the Scriptures.

The Catholic, however, does not believe in justification by faith alone, nor that a person can be saved apart from the instrumentality of the church. The Virgin Mary is in reality given a larger place than Christ is. It is also a help no know something of those saints of the Roman Catholic Church who are familiar to Protestants as well: Augustine, Francis Xavier, Madame Guyon--and to quote hymns by Father Faber, the author of "Souls of men, why will ye scatter," and many other beautiful hymns.
Some useful suggestions by Mrs. Turnbull are:

- Try to center conversation on Christ as much as possible.
- Stress the possibility and joy of being assured of salvation, and knowing the forgiveness of sins.
- Never seek to defend Protestantism.

- Do not dwell on the sins of the Roman clergy.
- Do not argue on the priority of Protestant or Roman Catholic Church, or as to whether Peter was the first Pope of Rome.
- Avoid appealing to history, as Roman Catholics have learned a very different account of the Reformation period.

A useful approach is to confess a high regard for the Virgin Mary, and ask the person if he believes he should do as the Virgin commanded. The answer will, of course, be in the affirmative. **Then quote Jo 2:5: "Whatsoever He saith unto you, do it," following this up by saying that He said: "Ye must be born again" (Jo 3:3).** The way is then clear to urge the necessity of regeneration. Show what regeneration is from 2Co 5:17. Distinguish baptism from regeneration by reading

1 Corinthians 1:14 (KJV)
[14] I thank God that I baptized none of you, but Crispus and Gaius; **1 Corinthians 4:15 (KJV)**
[15] For though ye have ten thousand instructors in Christ, yet *have ye* not many fathers: for in Christ Jesus I have begotten you through the gospel. he baptism of Simon (Ac 8:13,21-23) did not regenerate him.

Show further that salvation is not by works (Ro 4:5 2Tim 1:9 Ep 2:8,9). Show him that those who become sons of God by receiving Christ may enjoy assurance of salvation (1Jo 5:13 Jo 10:27-29 Ac 13:38,39).

Urge the necessity of confession, first of sins to God (1Jo 1:9); then of Christ to men (Ro 10:9-10). Show that there is ONLY ONE MEDIATOR between God and men--Christ (1Ti 2:5).

Since the Bible is largely banned to the Roman Catholic, encourage him to read his Bible, for "the entrance of thy word giveth light."

UNITARIANISM

The denial of the deity of Christ--and consequently of the Trinity Jesus was merely a good man, the Holy Spirit, an influence. The atonement is unnecessary, since sin is merely a defect which education will remove. The Bible is neither inspired nor infallible. The supernatural is scorned. It is obvious that the task of the worker is to deal with the inquirer concerning the Person and work of Christ. Dr. Evans suggests the following method:

1. Show that he cannot have the Father without the Son (1Jo 2:22,23 Jo 14:6 Mt 11:27). To disown the Son is to shut the door of knowledge of the Father.

2. Show that salvation comes in no other way, save through the person and work of Jesus Christ (Ac 4:12). If Christ is rejected, what then? (Jo 8:21,24).

3. Show that it is God's will that men should believe on His Son (Jo 5:22,23 Php 2:9).

4. The awful guilt resting on one who rejects Jesus Christ as his Savior (Jo 16:8-10 1Jo 5:10-12 Heb 10:28,29).

5. If necessary prove from Scripture the deity of Christ Divine names (Ac 3:14 Jo 20:28); divine attributes (Mr 2:8 Mt 18:20 Jo 1:1), divine works (Jo 1:1-3 Col 1:16); and divine worship (Mt 14:33 28:9), are ascribed to Him.

How to lead a Muslim to Christ

1). Point out that there are some similarities between Christianity and Islam: Both are monotheistic. Both believe that Adam and Eve were the parents of the human race. Both believe in the existence of prophets, and both affirm the validity of some of the same prophets. Both believe in the existence of angels. Both believe in a coming day of judgment. Each system claims a special revelation from God.

2). Point out that that radical distinctions exist between these two systems. Islam affirms that Allah is the only god and that Mohammed is his prophet. Scripture affirms that Jesus is the way to God (John 17:3) and that He is the capstone of God's revelation to man (Heb. 1:1-3). Islam denies that man is a sinner. It denies any doctrine of original sin. Islam denies the Trinity, and specifically the deity of Christ. Islam denies that Christ died and rose again. It affirms that Allah caught Christ up to heaven. Islam favors theocracy, whereas the Bible endorses the separation of church and state. Islam teaches that when the anti-Christ appears, Jesus will save the Muslim cause. Christians expect that Jesus will return to rule over all and to judge those who have not believed on Him.

3. Explain that Allah is not the same god as Jehovah. From the over 300 idols and gods in the Kaaba, Mohammed chose the moon god, Allah, to be the one supreme and only true deity (hence the crescent). "Allah" is not a common name for deity, and an Arab must use another name to signify any other god. Christians should not speak of their God as Allah, but should use Yahweh, the God of Israel, the God and Father of Jesus, etc.

4. A clear profession of personal faith in the Lord Jesus Christ is important, acknowledging Jesus as Lord and Savior, and that there is no salvation but by Him.

5. New believers are to be baptized, to meet regularly with other believers (this may need to be done with great discretion), and to take communion.

6. Believers should be encouraged to read the Old Testament and the New Testament to offset false teaching from the past.

7. Christian concepts must be clearly defined. Sin must be seen as something that is so serious in its consequences that it necessitated the incarnation and the atoning sacrifice of Christ. Yahweh must be seen as One who is holy and yet Self-giving. The Christian concept of the Trinity will need definition and explanation, including

admission that it presents problems to the human intellect.

8. New believers should renounce and forsake occultism and harmful Islamic practices (i.e., shamanism, prayers to saints, use of charms, curses, incantations, mistreatment of women, revenge, etc.).

9. A few Muslim practices and traditions (e.g. fasting, alms, circumcision, wearing the head covering, refraining from pork and alcohol, etc.) may at times be done out of respect for family or neighbors, but not as acts thought necessary to receive forgiveness of sin. Continuation of most Muslim practices is inappropriate.

10. As anywhere else, new believers are to show evidence of the new birth and growth in grace, not just forsaking past practices.

CHRISTIAN SCIENCE

Let the worker have some idea of what Mrs. Eddy, the high priestess of the cult, teaches. **The following statements are quoted from her book SCIENCE AND HEALTH, 1906 edition:**

"GOD is 'divine principle ... not personal (cf. Is 43:3). CHRIST 'is incorporeal, spiritual, the offspring of Mary's self-conscious communion with God" (cf. 1Ti 2:5). The Holy Spirit is 'divine science' (cf. Jo 14:16). It was impossible for MAN 'never born and never dying to fall from his high estate' (cf. 1Ti 2:14 A.S.V.). 'Whatever indicates the fall of man--is the Adam dream.' 'Man is incapable of SIN' (cf. 1Jo 1:9 Ro 3:23). As to ATONEMENT, 'one sacrifice, however great, is insufficient to pay the debt of sin' (of which she has told us man is incapable) (cf. Heb 9:26). The DEVIL is 'a lie, belief in sin, sickness and death' (cf. Mt 4:3,4). 'There is no MATTER' (cf. Gen 1:1) 'Man is never SICK' (cf. Ja 5:14). 'Man is incapable of DEATH' (cf. Heb 9:27). PRAYER: 'The habit of pleading with the divine mind as one pleads with a human being ... is an error which impedes spiritual growth' (cf. Mt 6:9 Jo 15:7)."

To perceive the origin of Christian Science, read 1Jo 4:1-3, for it denies that "Jesus Christ is come in the flesh." The Christian Scientist accepts the Scriptures as inspired (albeit claiming the same inspiration for SCIENCE AND HEALTH), so the worker has something to go on.

Ask the seeker to whom he prays, if God is not a person. Can he pray to a principle? Seeing he does not believe in a personal devil, ask how evil originated. If the Devil is only a lie, can a lie be punished? (Rev 20:10). If man is incapable of death, ask if he would stand up and allow someone to shoot him. Having shown the untruth of Christian Science from the Scriptures given above, and unveiled some of its fallacies by the questioning method, lead him to Christ, the Sinless Substitute (2Co 5:21 Gal 3:13 1Pe 2:24 Heb 9:22). To prove that curing of sickness is no proof of divine origin, use Mt 7:22,23 2Th 2:8,9.

UNIVERSALISTS

They are those who believe that all men will be saved in the final restoration of all things. The arguments to use with deniers of Hell have already been given. Their main Scriptures are ITi 2:3,4 1Co 15:22. The former expresses the desire of God's heart, but not His decree. Man's will is the determining factor. The latter verse read in its context, deals not with the reception of eternal life, but with physical resurrection.

The part played by man's will is seen in Lu 13:3 Jo 5:40. Such Scriptures as 2Th 1:7-9 Mt 25:41-46 Rev 20:15 21:8 clearly show that all men will not be finally saved.

JEWS

To deal effectively with Jews, the worker must have a good working knowledge of the Old Testament, and of the place of the Jews in God's plan.

1. Show how Christ fulfilled the Old Testament prophecies concerning the Messiah. A Jew (Gen 28:13,14). Of tribe of Judah (Mic 5:2). Of the family of David (Isa 11:1-10 Jer 23:5,6). Born of a virgin (Isa 7:14). In Bethlehem (Mic 5:2). Rejected and crucified (Ps 22:1). Before the destruction of the Temple (Dan 9:26). His coming to be in humility (Isa 53), and in glory (Ze 2:5).

2. Show that the Old Testament sacrifices were done away in Christ and that salvation is found only in His shed blood (Heb. 8:10 ; cf. Lev 17:11 Jo 1:29). Show also that Moses spoke of Christ (Jo 5:45-47).

3. Warn of the punishment meted out to those who reject Christ (Heb 10:26-29).

If a Jew objects that "God did not marry a woman to give birth to Christ," answer that God is a miracle-working God (Cf.gen. 18:14 Lu 1:37. Also Lu 1:26-32 Mt 1:18-25). If he contends that the worship of Jesus is worshiping a man, use Gen 18:1,2 (where one of the men was Jehovah), and Jos 5:13-15. The objection that the doctrine of the Trinity teaches three Gods instead of one, may be answered by Gen 1:1, where "God," Elohim, is plural. See also Gen 1:26 ("us," "our,"). If he objects that Is 53:1 refers not to Christ but to suffering Israel, show that this is impossible, since the One who suffers is suffering, not for His own sins, but for those of another (Is 53:4,5,8), and that other is suffering Israel!

One who would work among Jews should be especially familiar with the Epistle to the Hebrews.

Russellism or Millenial Dawn, or JEHOVAH'S WITNESSES

This chameleon-like cult is flourishing greatly today. It was founded by Pastor C. T. Russell, and is perpetuated today in word and writing by Judge Rutherford. In addition to the three aliases given above, this cult masquerades as "The International Bible Students' Association," "Metropolitan Pulpit," "Zion's Watch-tower," etc.

DOCTRINES It denies the deity and humanity of Christ, He being the highest order of created being. Scriptures to answer this have already been given. Christ, they say, at death became extinct, body and soul, and His body was not raised (cf. Lu 24:39). He is now a disembodied spirit, for His body passed off in gases in the tomb. He returned to the world in 1874, and the Millenium began in 1914 (cf. Acts 1:11 1Ti 3:16). The Holy Spirit is merely an influence (cf. Jo 16:13,14). A second probation after death is promised, a promise which is distinctly countermanded by Lu 16:19-31 (cf. Rev 22:11 2Cor 6:2 Jo 5:28,29). Those who die become extinct, but are raised again (a difficult process surely!) in the next age. (See Mt 10:28 Php 1:23 2Cor 5:8)

The Scriptures given under "Christian Science" will answer several of the above errors.

SPIRITISM

That disembodied spirits can communicate with the living is clear from Scripture (1Sa 28:11-20), but the curse of God rests on the devotees of Spiritism. The existence of Satan and angels is denied. The worker should not commence by making the sweeping assertion that the whole thing is of the Devil, true though that is, or he will lose his point of contact with his "prospect."

The first thing to do is to show what the Bible teaches concerning God's attitude to Spiritism (1Ch 10:13,14 Is 8:19,20 1Jo 4:1-3 2Th 2:9-12).

Next show from Lu 16:1 that Spiritism is not the work of spirits of the dead, for there it is made clear that the spirits of departed ones have no communication with earth, that being absolutely forbidden by the Scriptures (De 18:9-12). Spiritism is a repudiation of God's revelation in His Word (Is 8:19,20). More credence is given to the supposed words of departed spirits than to the Word of God (Lu 16:31).

To test the origin of these spirit impersonations, use 1Jo 4:1-3. The Christian can expect these special manifestations of evil spirits in these last days (1Ti 4:1,2,6).

The main errors involved in Spiritism are: Denial of the personality of GOD, the deity of CHRIST, in making Him only a medium; dishonoring the HOLY SPIRIT; denial of the ATONEMENT, future JUDGMENT or punishment of sin; and the SECOND ADVENT of Christ.

Dr. Riley tells of Charles Dickens attending a number of séances and being almost convinced and ready to become a Spiritist, when at a certain one he asked the medium to speak with Lindley Murray. A spook appeared, and Dickens said: "Are you Lindley Murray?" The spook replied: "I are!" "Excuse me," said Dickens, "Lindley may have his faults, but he is a good grammarian," and so he departed, to have no more to do with Spiritism.

THEOSOPHY

As in the case of other cults, there is much that is false in this esoteric philosophy. The BIBLE is only one of many other Bibles of equal authority. Their idea of God is pantheistic. CHRIST is ONE of the manifestations of the Logos. MAN has one spirit, three souls, a life principle, and two bodies, and is subject to reincarnation. SALVATION is by works, the Theosophist trying all the time to "make good Karma" or to pile up merit.

The basic error is the place given to the Scriptures, and the worker must first show the preeminence of God's Word as previously shown. (Use 2Ti 3:16 Heb 4:12 Mt 5:18.) As to the personality of God, see Gen 17:1 Ps 103:13. The deity and uniqueness of Christ may be shown from Jo 1:1 Heb

1:3. Instead of being a compound personality, as taught by Theosophists, man is a being created in the image of God, fallen, but subject to redemption and resurrection, not to reincarnation. Man cannot obtain salvation on the ground of his own merit (Ro 3:20 Tit 3:5 Ep 2:8,9). Instead of man's goal and destiny being the nebulous nirvana, it is a prepared place in the Father's house (Jo 14:2).

SEVENTH DAY ADVENTISM

This is one of the most subtle of the cults, because it has more semblance of a spiritual basis. As the name suggests, its key teaching is the observance of the old Jewish Sabbath, instead of the first day of the week--an indispensable condition of salvation. The mark of the Beast is the nonobservance of the Sabbath. Dr. Evans suggests the following method of attack:

1. Know their favorite passages and show how they wrongly interpret them, e.g., 1Jo 2:4. Show from 1Jo 3:23 that the commandment referred to is love and faith, not Sabbath-keeping. "Commandments" in Re 22:14 is made to refer to the Ten Commandments, but these words are omitted entirely from the American Standard Version.

2. Show, then, that the law (including the Sabbath) is done away (2Co 3:7-11). These verses teach that one is either under the old covenant with its curse or under the new covenant with its blessing. If one keeps the Sabbath, it is an acknowledgment of being under the former, and thus excluded from the benefits of the latter.

3. Show that by the death of Christ Christians have become dead to the law (Ro 7:1-4 10:3-9).

4. Stress the fact that every one of the Ten Commandments, except the fourth, is reaffirmed in the New Testament. Nowhere is the Church of Christ commanded to keep the Sabbath.

5. Show that the Sabbath is a purely Jewish institution, never meant to be binding on a Christian (De 5:12-15). It was a sign between Israel and God (Ex 31:13-17).

6. Show that there is no scriptural warrant for their theory that the soul sleeps between death and the resurrection. (See 2Co 5:1-8 Php 1:20-23.) Some of the Scriptures they use in this connection are Ac 2:34. But verses 29 and 31 (Ac 2:29,31) have clear reference to the body, not the soul of David (Ec 9:5-10). "The dead know nothing"--but the context limits this to "under the sun". The same words are used in 1Sa 20:39 1Ti 6:4, but do not bear the meaning Adventists put on them. Da 12:2 with Jo 11:11,14,39. Note that of Lazarus it was said, "He now stinketh." Did this refer to his soul or his body? By taking their proof texts in their context and with parallel passages, it will be easily proved that their contentions are unscriptural.

7. Show that the Scriptures teach that the spirit or soul does not die with the body (Ec 12:7 3:21 1Co 5:5 Lu 23:43-46 Ac 7:59 Mt 10:28).

It is well to know that the observance of the first day is of neither Romish nor heathen origin, as they contend. They lay

this change of day at the door of the pope of Rome. The early Church Fathers, writing in the first and second centuries--Ignatius, Justin Martyr, Clement, and many others--all testify to the fact that the observance of the first day of the week was general.

Again, it is physically impossible for Adventists the world over to observe the Jewish Sabbath from sunset to sunset. In the far north the sun does not set for weeks. In going round the world westward, a day is lost, and in going the opposite way, a day is gained. It is perfectly obvious that the commandment was a purely local one.

In dealing with Adventists, the worker will find that they are very bigoted and will try to monopolize the conversation. Stipulate that you will answer questions in turn, or they will evade the issue when faced with convincing and unanswerable Scriptures.

Oh, matchless honor, all unsought, High privilege, surpassing thought, That Thou shouldest call me, Lord to be Linked in such work, O God, with Thee! To carry out Thy wondrous plan, To bear Thy message unto man; In trust with Christ's own Word of grace To each soul of the human race.

I think it unfortunate that Judaism is lumped in with "cults," since it is a world religion rather than a cult.

MISCELLANEOUS SUGGESTIONS

"Suffer the little children to come unto me." The soul-winner must emulate his Exemplar in not ignoring little children, "for of such is the kingdom of heaven." Such a subject is deserving of a volume to itself, but this study must necessarily be confided to a few of the more important issues. Dr. Torrey once said: "No other form of Christian work brings such immediate, such large, and such lasting results as work for the conversion of children." It was Spurgeon's opinion that "capacity for believing lies more in the child than in the man." (See Mt 18:6.)

Parents are, of course, God's own appointed teachers of the child, and the religious training cannot be done by proxy. The parent who neglects this duty is unwittingly robbing himself of the highest privilege this world affords. Why should the winning of the child, whom the parent has brought into the world, be left to a stranger?

The late Rev. Joseph W. Kemp made the seven following suggestions for successful work among children:

1. **THERE MUST BE A THOROUGH BELIEF** in the child's need. The child, no less than the man or woman, is "dead in trespasses and sins," and unless there is a clear sense of the utter ruin and spiritual death of children, there will be no power to bring blessing to them. We believe, of course, in the salvation of infants who have not reached the years of moral accountability, but even these can accept Christ as Savior.

2. **THERE MUST BE A CONSCIOUSNESS OF ONE'S MISSION**--not to amuse or instruct only, but to secure the salvation of the child.

3. **THERE MUST BE RELIANCE ON THE SPIRIT'S POWER** as much with children as with adults.

4. **THERE MUST BE ADAPTATION TO THE CHILD.** We need our best and most industrious studies and our ripest powers to save the children.

5.   **WE MUST USE THE CHILD'S LANGUAGE**--not baby talk, but language the child can understand.

6.   **WE MUST NOT EXPECT TOO MUCH OF THE CHILD**--an ever-present danger with us grownups. Don't expect the child to abandon its childish ways and become a mature old man!

7.   **WE MUST EXERCISE PATIENCE.** It will be easier to do this if we remember our own stumbling progress.

The worker among children must exercise wisdom in making an appeal, as it is a very simple thing to get the whole class or audience to respond to the appeal. It is a mistake never to make an appeal, but an equally great mistake to make appeals continually, for the child-heart easily becomes accustomed and hardened to them. One of our evangelists invites children present at his meetings, if they desire to accept Christ as Savior, to go home, write their name in Jo 3:16 instead of THE WORLD and "WHOSOEVER," and mail or hand it to him the next day. This avoids the dangers of a mass movement.

Remember that Moody was converted at 14, Fanny Crosby at 11, Jonathan Edwards at 7, Isaac Watts at 9, and that 90 per cent of Christians are saved before they reach eighteen years of age.

Chapter 13

TRACT DISTRIBUTION

The widespread use of tracts and literature by the false cults should arouse the Christian worker to the great possibilities for good of the distribution of suitable tracts. Souls who would never darken a church door will often read a tract. Here are some suggestions as to the most effective methods of tract work.

1. Have well written and attractively printed tracts which you have read yourself. Always carry some with you.

2. Know your tracts, and endeavor to suit the tract to the recipient, e.g., do not give a sailor a tract dealing with railways, or do not give a tract on holiness to a sinner.

3. Be courteous, genial, and tactful in your approach. If rebuffed, manifest the love of Christ. Even if those you approach refuse to read your tract, they will certainly read you.

4. Not every tract is suitable for indiscriminate distribution.

5. Be prayerful and confident of God's blessing.

6. Follow up the opening which the giving of the tract has made, with a word on the way of salvation.

7. Distribute tracts in public places, from house to house, in hospitals, in letter boxes, on sports grounds, in vacant automobiles, confident that some of the seed thus sown will bring forth fruit.

AS AN ENCOURAGEMENT TO THE TRACT DISTRIBUTER,

A story of remarkable blessing resulting from the giving of a tract follows. A tract by Dr. Richard Gibbs was handed by a peddler to Richard Baxter, whose CALL TO THE UNCONVERTED fell into the hands of Philip Doddridge, the great preacher and hynm-writer. He wrote THE RISE AND PROGRESS OF RELIGION, by means of which William Wilberforce, the emancipator of the slaves, was converted. He in turn wrote PRACTICAL CHRISTIANITY, which fired the heart of Leigh Richmond, who wrote THE DAIRYMAN'S DAUGHTER, of which, before 1848, 4,000,000 were circulated in fifty languages. Wilberforce's book also fell into the hands of Thomas Chalmers, and was the means of bringing him out into the light of the Gospel, and all Scotland rang with his mighty eloquence.

Do not despise the ministry of the GOOD tract.

A CONSECRATED PEN

Who can measure the blessing which has flowed from a consecrated pen? Have you ever prayed: "Lord, sanctify my pen to Thy use?" Pray it now.

Let's Go Soul Winning

Some timid Christian who is not courageous enough to talk to someone face to face about Christ, could at least use his pen. Dr. H. Clay Trumbull, the greatest soul-winner of his day, was converted through a letter written him by a college mate who had not the courage to speak to him personally.

The same fruitful avenue of service is open to the invalid or to the mother whose children are away from home. The letter will probably be read and reread, whereas a spoken word might be forgotten.

1. Pray before and after writing each letter.

2. Write lovingly, sympathetically and simply, adding your testimony to the Scriptures you quote.

3. Having put the way of salvation clearly, urge the recipient to definitely decide to accept Christ at once.

4. Enclose a suitable tract, or perhaps a decision card.

5. Write to one who has recently decided, one who has backslidden, one who is passing through trial and testing, to a lonely boy or girl.

6. Do not wait for a reply, necessarily, before you write again. All are not good correspondents.

Most workers, Sunday school teachers, Bible club leaders, and Christian workers do not exploit the power of the pen nearly as much as they should.

Only a note, yes, only a note to a friend in a distant land. The Spirit said "Write!" but then you had planned Some different work, and you thought It mattered little, you did not know 'T would have saved a soul from sin and woe, You were out of touch with your Lord.

Chapter 14

Follow Up

INSTRUCTION FOR CONVERTS

Many a promising convert has made no progress in the new life, simply because he was not correctly instructed at the time of his conversion. It is not wise to overload the newly-born babe with sage advice, but several things should be made crystal clear to him.

1. To be a happy Christian he must confess Christ to men at the earliest possible moment, preferably to his own people and then to his work-mates (Ro 10:9-10). He must be out and out for God to experience God's best. The would-be secret disciple never knows the real joy of the Lord. Explain that if he trusts his newly-found Savior, He will give him the power to testify (Php 4:13).

2. Show that Christ is not only his Savior but his Lord
Romans 10:9 (KJV)
⁹ That if thou shalt confess with thy mouth the Lord Jesus, and shalt believe in thine heart that God hath raised him from the dead, thou shalt be saved.

3. Urge him to read the Bible every day, and if first thing in the morning, asking the Holy Spirit to make the Book live. Explain that the Bible is to the spiritual life what

bread is to the physical life, and that he cannot grow without food.

4. Having heard God's voice in the Bible, instruct him to let God hear his voice in prayer, to pour out his soul and his desires before God (Mt 6:6). Make clear his privilege to talk with God and walk with God every hour of the day, and to claim the fulfillment of His promises. Encourage the habit of ejaculatory prayer throughout the day as well as the time spent in the secret place.

5. Advise him to begin to work for Christ, and endeavor to serve Him.

6. JOHN 1:38-41 (KJV) **BIBLICAL DISCIPLESHIP**
   [38] THEN JESUS TURNED, AND SAW THEM FOLLOWING, AND SAITH UNTO THEM, WHAT SEEK YE? THEY SAID UNTO HIM, RABBI, (WHICH IS TO SAY, BEING INTERPRETED, MASTER,) WHERE DWELLEST THOU?
   [39] HE SAITH UNTO THEM, COME AND SEE. THEY CAME AND SAW WHERE HE DWELT, AND ABODE WITH HIM THAT DAY: FOR IT WAS ABOUT THE TENTH HOUR.
   [40] ONE OF THE TWO WHICH HEARD JOHN *SPEAK*, AND FOLLOWED HIM, WAS ANDREW, SIMON PETER'S BROTHER.
   [41] HE FIRST FINDETH HIS OWN BROTHER SIMON, AND SAITH UNTO HIM, WE HAVE FOUND THE MESSIAS, WHICH IS, BEING INTERPRETED, THE CHRIST.

   WHAT DO YOU KNOW ABOUT THE NEW CONVERT? HAVE A 3X5 CARD WITH THE FOLLOWING INFORMATION ON IT TO FILL OUT

   - NAME
   - ADDRESS
   - PHONE NUMBER

- AGE
- MARRIED
- CHILDREN
- E-MAIL ADDRESS
- WHAT DO YOU LIKE TO DO?
- CHURCH AFFILIATION

THE MOST IMPORTANT QUESTION YOU NEED TO ASK THE PERSON.

NOW THAT YOU HAVE REPENTED OF YOUR SIN, DO YOU REALLY WANT TO FOLLOW CHRIST?
YES

NO

- IF YES, IT IS IMPORTANT TO MAKE APPOINTMENT WITH THEM.
- IF YOU ARE IN A HOME, YOU NEED TO ASK IF YOU CAN COME BACK AND TALK WITH THEM LATER.
- BE CAREFUL TO NOT WEAR YOUR WELCOME OUT
- DON'T BE PUSSHY.. PRAISE THEM FOR THE DECISION THEY HAVE MADE. SET A TIME AND DATE TO RETURN.

IT IS IMPORTANT TO FOLLOW UP
- BE CONSISTENT
- LET THE PERSON KNOW YOU CARE ABOUT THEM
- ASK IF YOU CAN PRAY WITH THEM
- DON'T BE IN A HURRY, DO NOT KEEP THEM TO LONG.
- GIVE THEM YOUR E-MAIL ADDRESS AND TELEPHONE NUMBER

- IF YOU ARE SOUL, WINNING AND YOU KNOW YOU CANNOT GET BACK TO SEE THEM...ASK IF YOU CAN HAVE A FRIEND CALL THEM OR E-MAIL THEM TO COME BY AND SEE THEM.
- REMEMBER, YOU ARE A NEW FACE AND THEY WILL NOT TRUST YOU AT FIRST. SO DO NOT BE PUSHY OR TO BOLD.

FOLLOW UP

- YOU SEND THEM A E-MAIL OR LETTER AS SOON AS POSSIBLE.
- YOU CAN CALL THEM ON THE PHONE AND ASK THEM HOW THEY ARE DOING. BUILD A FRIENDSHIP
- REMEMBER THE CULTS USE THIS PROCESS AND ARE VERY GOOD AT STEALING NEW CONVERTS.
- BEFORE YOU MAKE THE SECOND HOUSE CALL, CALL THEM AND ASK THEM TO WRITE DOWN ANY QUESTIONS THEY MAY HAVE.
- BE PATIENT AND CARING BUT, NOT OVER CARING.
- BRING WITH YOU INFORMATION ABOUT YOUR CHURCH
- ASK THEM IF THEY HAVE SEEN ANY CHANGES IN THEIR LIFE SINCE BECOMING A CHRISTIAN.
- SHOW THEM SCRIPTURE ACTS 8:26-38 THE STORY OF PHILIP AND THE EUNIC.. THIS IS A GREAT ICE-BREAKER FOR BAPTISM.

GREAT VERSES ON BAPTISM
- MT 3:7; MT 20:22-23; MT 21:25; MR 1:4; MR 10:38-39; MR 11:30; LU 3:3; LU 7:29; LU 12:50; LU 20:4; AC 1:22; AC 10:37; AC 13:24; AC 18:25; AC 19:3-4; RO 6:4; EPH 4:5; COL 2:12; 1PE 3:21

WHAT NEXT?

- BY NOW YOU HAVE MADE A FRIEND OR A ACQUAINTANCE.
- ASK THE PERSON IF YOU CAN MEET AGAIN WITH THEM.
- IF THE PERSON SAYS YES, YOU ARE ON YOUR WAY TO TRUE DISCIPLESHIP.
- ASK THEM IF THEY WOULD BE YOUR GUEST AT CHURCH AND MAKE SURE, YOU SIT WITH THEM WHEN THEY COME TO CHURCH.
- WHEN THE INVITATION IS GIVEN ASK IF THEY WOULD LIKE TO GO DOWN AND MAKE THEIR DECISION PUBLIC.

CHURCH MEMBERSHIP

- YOUR CHURCH HAS A CONSTITUTION AND IT IS IMPORTANT TO EXPLAIN WHAT IS REQUIRED AT YOUR CHURCH FOR MEMBERSHIP.
- ONCE THEY FOLLOW UP AND PUBLICLY, MAKE IT KNOWN THEY ARE A CHRISTIAN. SHOWING THEM THE BIBLICAL BASIS FOR MEMBERSHIP IS IMPORTANT.

Let's Go Soul Winning

Practical Principles in Soul Winning

By

Dr. David N. Smeltz Sr.

Class Lessons

40 hour

INTRODUCTION

This course is designed to train you in the art of witnessing to someone with the Gospel of Christ. It will be practical and pointed.

We will hope to secure four things

Our Goal   to be an affective witness

Our Guide   The Bible

Our Going   House to House

Memorizing scripture

You will a quiz each night accept for the first and the last night.

You will have a final exam.

Each class will be taped..

Good luck as we study the word of God to be soul winners.

Proverbs 11:30 (KJV)
^{30} The fruit of the righteous *is* a tree of life; and he that winneth souls *is* wise.

Lesson 1

Soul Winning Made Easy

THE VALUE OF A SOUL

How can we compute the value of a soul?

1.   BY ITS NATURE AND ORIGIN

    a.

2.   BY ITS POWERS AND CAPACITIES

    a.

3.   BY THE DURATION OF ITS EXISTENCE

    a.

    b.

    c.

    d.

    e.

f.

4.   BY THE COST OF ITS REDEMPTION

a.

5.   BY THE STRUGGLE REQUIRED FOR ITS POSSESSION

a.

b

c

The Big Question, HOW MAY THIS "CONCERN" BE OBTAINED

- It is not a natural and inevitable product of the heart.
- It is not produced by a fresh resolution to be concerned about souls.
- It will be produced in the heart only by using the means adapted to stir up our minds on the subject. Paul's concern for souls, as one has said, sprang from a threefold conviction.

First,

Second,

Third,

A STRIKING EXAMPLE

I.   **ABSENCE OF CONCEPTION OF THE VALUE OF A SOUL**

Homework Read John 1-4
NOTES

Lesson 2

THE FITNESS OF THE WORKER

I. AN UNWAVERING PURPOSE

WHENEVER I WAS IN SUCH INTIMACY WITH A SOUL AS TO BE JUSTIFIED IN CHOOSING MY THEME OF CONVERSATION, THE THEME OF THEMES SHOULD HAVE PROMINENCE BETWEEN US,

II. AN UNASSAILABLE ASSURANCE OF HIS OWN SALVATION

III. A WORKING KNOWLEDGE OF THE SCRIPTURES

To summarize in the words of Dr. Torrey:

1. .

2.

3.

4.

To these we would add:

5

IV. A HABITUALLY PRAYERFUL ATTITUDE

V. A LOVINGLY TACTFUL APPROACH

"Certainly, that is characteristic of Britons verywhere."

Will just as soon as I see a real occasion for it."

> All this was done in a playful way, but the result of his tactful approach was that they kept their profanity bottled up for the rest of the voyage.

V.   THE ENDUEMENT WITH POWER

Homework Read Romans 3
NOTES

Lesson 3

THE PLACE OF PRAYER IN SOUL-WINNING

HE IS COUNTING ON YOU

What Next? "PRAYER"

WE MUST BE SURE THAT WE ARE STANDING ON PRAYING GROUND.

FIRST: for MORAL COURAGE TO SPEAK FOR CHRIST WHEN OPPORTUNITY OFFERS

SECOND, FOR GUIDANCE AS TO WHOM TO APPROACH.

THIRD, FOR GUIDANCE AS TO WHAT TO SAY.   The worker's prayer for the soul to be won will also be threefold.

FIRST: THAT ANY INDIFFERENCE OR HOSTILITY MAY BE BROKEN DOWN AND AN OPENING MADE FOR DELIVERING THE MESSAGE OF SALVATION.

SECOND: THAT THE SOIL OF THE HEART MAY BE PREPARED FOR THE SOWING OF THE SEED

THIRD: THAT THE SOUL MAY BE LIBERATED FROM THE POWER OF SATAN.

LORD, TEACH US TO PRAY

David N. Smeltz

Homework Read Romans 6

NOTES

Lesson 4

DO'S AND DON'TS FOR THE SOUL-WINNER

1. DO BELIEVE GOD'S PROMISE OF WISDOM (Ja 1:5).

2. DO CLAIM DELIVERANCE FROM THE FEAR OF MAN.

3. DO KEEP YOUR EYES OPEN FOR OPPORTUNITIES.

4   DO PURPOSE TO WIN ONE SOUL.

WIN ONE SOUL

   I will seek, with God's help, to win one

   Soul each year, and endeavor to get them

   To do the same

Name …………………

SOME DON'TS

   1. DON'T LET IT BE APPARENT THAT YOU ARE A PERSONAL WORKER.

2. **DON'T ATTEMPT TO DEAL WITH MORE THAN ONE SOUL AT A TIME.** Get your "prospect"

3. **DON'T BE DRAWN INTO AN ARGUMENT**

4. **DON'T ATTRACT ATTENTION TO YOURSELF** or your experience. Seek to attract souls to your Lord.

5. **DON'T MONOPOLIZE THE CONVERSATION**

6. **DON'T AS A RULE DEAL WITH PERSONS OF THE OPPOSITE SEX.**

7. **DON'T AS A RULE CHOOSE A PERSON MUCH YOUR SENIOR TO DEAL**

8. **DON'T RELY ON YOUR OWN ABILITY**

9. **DON'T MULTIPLY TEXTS AND ILLUSTRATIONS.**

10. **DON'T BE UNDULY FAMILIAR**

11. **DON'T BECOME IMPATIENT**

12. **DON'T BREAK IN WHEN SOMEONE ELSE IS DEALING WITH A SOUL.**

13. **DON'T HURRY OR DO SHODDY WORK.**

14. **DON'T BE DISCOURAGED**

15. **DON'T FORGET**

The value of one soul, O Lord, Teach me to see; and as Thy Word Assures me of the awful fate Which doth the Christless soul await, Oh, may I wrestle and prevail With God and men, like Israel.

> *Give me Thy tenderness and tact, Guide every thought and word and act, And cause me so to do my part To reach the hard or longing heart, That men to Thee, O Christ, may turn, More of Thy tenderness to learn.*
>
> --Estelle Edmeades

Homework Pass out 20 tracks
NOTES

Lesson 5

AN OLD TESTAMENT ILLUSTRATION AND A NEW TESTAMENT EXAMPLE

THE OLD TESTAMENT ILLUSTRATION

The word WIN

I. **HIS QUALIFICATIONS**

    1.

    2.

II. **HIS MISSION**

    1. ABRAHAM REVEALED TO HIM HIS SECRET PURPOSE

    2. ELIEZER RECEIVED DEFINITE INSTRUCTIONS

    3. HE WAS ROBBED OF ALL HONOR, BUT FREED OF ALL RESPONSIBILITY.

III. **HIS ATTITUDE**

    1. HE DID NOT UNDERESTIMATE THE DIFFICULTY

    2. HE PROPOSED A CARNAL EXPEDIENT

3. HIS DEPENDENCE ON THE ANGEL DID NOT CUT THE NERVE OF HIS OWN ENDEAVORS.

4. HE SUBORDINATED HIS OWN COMFORT AND INTERESTS

IV. HIS METHOD

1. HE PRAYED before he made the proposal

2. HE DELIVERED HIS MESSAGE CLEARLY AND SIMPLY.

3. HE USED NO UNDUE PRESSURE,

4. HE EXPECTED SUDDEN SUCCESS.

Homework Witness to someone

NOTES

Lesson 6

THE NEW TESTAMENT EXAMPLE

Has it ever occurred to you that the greater part of the harvest of our Lord's earthly ministry was hand-gathered fruit? Seven out of the eleven apostles, and probably the other four as well, were won by individual appeal. In both Matthew and John, at least **SIXTEEN PRIVATE INTERVIEWS** are recorded for our instruction. Surely, this is sufficient evidence that the Master considered personal soul winning as of primary importance. In this, as in everything else, He is our Exemplar.

Christ was THE MASTER SOUL-WINNER. Knowing, as He did, what was in man (Jo 2:25), and the workings of the human mind which He had fashioned, His methods in dealing with various classes will be of the greatest interest and importance to His followers. Let us learn some lessons from Him.

1. **HE WAS NOT CLASS-CONSCIOUS.**

2. **HE MADE A TACTFUL APPROACH.**

3. **HE COMMENDED RATHER THAN CONDEMNED.**

4. **HE CONSTANTLY ILLUSTRATED**

5. **HE REFUSED TO BE DRAWN INTO PROFITLESS ARGUMENT.**

6. **HE WEPT AND PRAYED**

David N. Smeltz

7. **HE NEVER FAILED TO MAKE A PERSONAL APPLICATION OF HIS TEACHINGS**

8. **HIS BLAMELESS LIFE**

AN EXAMPLE

THE CASE--The Woman of Samaria (Jo 4)

(a)

(b)

(c)

(d)

(e)

THE METHOD

(a)

(b)

(c)

(d)

(e)

1.

2.

3

4

OPPORTUNITY, APPROACH, AND DIAGNOSIS

I. OPPORTUNITY

    1. IN THE HOME

    2. IN THE SUNDAY SCHOOL OR BIBLE CLASS

    3. AT AFTERNOON TEA PARTIES

    4. IN THE CHURCH

    5. IN TRAVEL

D. L. Moody made it the practice of his life to speak to men on the streetcars. It is related of him that in thus dealing with a man on a Detroit streetcar, he asked him the question: "Are you a Christian?" The man answered: "No, sir, but I wish I were." Mr. Moody there and then led the man to Christ. We don't have many street cars today, we do have buses and trains.

    6. AMONG YOUR OWN

Notes

Lesson 7

THE APPROACH

Be natural in manner and in tone of voice.

Study the art of diverting conversation to spiritual topics as did Jesus with the woman of Samaria.

THE DIAGNOSIS

The following story related by Howard W. Pope shows the importance of correct diagnosis.

NOTES

Lesson 8

CONVERTED PERSONS.

Those with whom you will come in contact, who need personal dealing, may be divided into two main classes: those who are open backsliders, and those whose Christian experience is unsatisfactory.

1. OPEN BACKSLIDERS

2. THOSE THAT CHRISTIAN EXPERIENCE HAS BEEN UNSATISFACTORY

    (a) NEGLECT OF PRAYER—

    (b) NEGLECT OF THE BIBLE

    (c) NEGLECT IN WITNESSING.

    (d) COMPROMISE WITH THE WORLD

    (e) ENSLAVED BY SIN

    (f) NO ASSURANCE OF SALVATION

A very general cause of lack of assurance is a dependence on feeling.

Lesson 9

UNCONVERTED PERSONS

These may be considered under five headings:

1. ANXIOUS OR INTERESTED.

WHAT IT IS TO BELIEVE

The final step is

It is well to emphasize the divine order--the fact, faith, and then feeling.

Jesus did it--on the cross.

God says it--in His Word.

I believe it--in my heart.

Feeling that you are saved cannot come before you ARE saved,

Go and find them ere they perish, Tell them of the Savior's love;
How He came to guide them safely To the Father's home above.
Go and find them in their darkness, Bound by chains of slavery;
Tell abroad the proclamation; Jesus Christ can set them free.
Go and find them, hasten! Hasten! Time is fleeting fast away;
They are dying, lost and hopeless while you linger day by day.

Lesson 10

THE INDIFFERENT OR CARELESS

    (a)   PRODUCE CONVICTION OF SIN.

    (b)   POINT TO CHRIST THE CRUCIFIED.

THOSE WHO HAVE RAISED OBJECTIONS OR HAVE DIFFICULTIES

1.
2
3
4

    (a) OBJECTIONS RELATING TO THE BIBLE OR ITS DOCTRINES

"THE BIBLE IS FULL OF CONTRADICTIONS."

"THE BIBLE IS IMPURE."

"NO SUCH BEING AS GOD EXISTS."

"THERE IS NO SUCH PLACE AS HELL

"GOD IS TOO LOVING TO CONDEMN ANYONE."

"THE BIBLE IS NOT INSPIRED."

OBJECTIONS BASED ON THE INCONSISTENCIES OF CHRISTIANS.

"THERE ARE TOO MANY HYPOCRITES IN THE CHURCH."

"I HAVE BEEN TREATED WRONGLY BY CHRISTIANS."

Lesson 11

PERSONAL DIFFICULTIES

"I AM NOT VERY BAD."

"I AM DOING MY BEST

"I GO TO CHURCH." OR "I HAVE BEEN CONFIRMED

"I HAVE ALWAYS BELIEVED IN CHRIST."

"I CANNOT BELIEVE

"I HAVE TRIED BEFORE AND FAILED."

"I AM TOO WEAK

"I WILL WAIT TILL I AM BETTER

"I AM TOO BAD."
"I'VE DONE NO ONE ANY HARM."

"I SEE NO HARM IN INNOCENT PLEASURES OF THE WORLD

"THERE IS TOO MUCH TO GIVE UP."

"I CAN'T GIVE UP MY SINS."

"I AM NOT YET READY TO COME."

"I WANT TO BE A CHRISTIAN, BUT I DON'T KNOW WHAT TO DO."

"I HAVE SOUGHT CHRIST, BUT HAVE NOT FOUND HIM." "I AM AFRAID OF PERSECUTION."

"I GUESS I'LL GET TO HEAVEN ALL RIGHT

"I WILL LOSE MY FRIENDS

"THE CHRISTIAN LIFE IS TOO HARD."

"I HAVE NO FEELING."

"I HAVE COMMITTED THE UNPARDONABLE SIN."

Lesson 12

WORKING AMONG FALSE CULTS

ROMAN CATHOLICISM

Since the Bible is largely banned to the Roman Catholic, encourage him to read his Bible, for "the entrance of thy word giveth light."

UNITARIANISM

1.

2.

3.

4.

5.

How to lead a Muslim to Christ

1.

2.

3.

4.

5.

6.

7.

8.

9.

10.

David N. Smeltz

CHRISTIAN SCIENCE

Let the worker have some idea of what Mrs. Eddy, the high priestess of the cult, teaches. **The following statements are quoted from her book SCIENCE AND HEALTH, 1906 edition:**

UNIVERSALISTS

JEWS

1.

2.

3.

One who would work among Jews should be especially familiar with the Epistle to the Hebrews.

Russellism or Millenial Dawn, or JEHOVAH'S WITNESSES

DOCTRINES

The Scriptures given under "Christian Science" will answer several of the above errors.

SPIRITISM

THEOSOPHY

SEVENTH DAY ADVENTISM

This is one of the most subtle of the cults, because it has more semblance of a spiritual basis. As the name suggests, its key teaching is the observance of the old Jewish Sabbath, instead of the first day of the week--an indispensable condition of salvation. The mark of the Beast is the nonobservance of the Sabbath. Dr. Evans suggests the following method of attack:

1.

2.

3.

4.

5.

6.

7.

It is well to know that the observance of the first day is of neither Romish nor heathen origin, as they contend. They lay this change of day at the door of the pope of Rome. The early Church Fathers, writing in the first and second centuries--Ignatius, Justin Martyr, Clement, and many others--all testify to the fact that the observance of the first day of the week was general.

MISCELLANEOUS SUGGESTIONS

1. THERE MUST BE A THOROUGH BELIEF

2. THERE MUST BE A CONSCIOUSNESS OF ONE'S MISSION—

3. THERE MUST BE RELIANCE ON THE SPIRIT'S POWER

4. THERE MUST BE ADAPTATION TO THE CHILD.

5. WE MUST USE THE CHILD'S LANGUAGE

6. WE MUST NOT EXPECT TOO MUCH OF THE CHILD--

7. WE MUST EXERCISE PATIENCE.

Lesson 13

TRACT DISTRIBUTION

The widespread use of tracts and literature by the false cults should arouse the Christian worker to the great possibilities for good of the distribution of suitable tracts. Souls who would never darken a church door will often read a tract. Here are some suggestions as to the most effective methods of tract work.

1.

2.

3.

4.

5.

6.

7.

AS AN ENCOURAGEMENT TO THE TRACT DISTRIBUTER,

David N. Smeltz

Do not despise the ministry of the GOOD tract.

A CONSECRATED PEN

1.

2.

3.

4.   .

5.

6.   .

David N. Smeltz

Lesson 14

Follow Up

INSTRUCTION FOR CONVERTS

Many a promising convert has made no progress in the new life, simply because he was not correctly instructed at the time of his conversion. It is not wise to overload the newly-born babe with sage advice, but several things should be made crystal clear to him.

1.

2.

3.

4.

5.

6.

WHAT DO YOU KNOW ABOUT THE NEW CONVERT? HAVE A 3X5 CARD WITH THE FOLLOWING INFORMATION ON IT TO FILL OUT

- NAME

David N. Smeltz

- ADDRESS
- PHONE NUMBER
- AGE
- MARRIED
- CHILDREN
- E-MAIL ADDRESS
- WHAT DO YOU LIKE TO DO?
- CHURCH AFFILIATION

THE MOST IMPORTANT QUESTION YOU NEED TO ASK THE PERSON.

NOW THAT YOU HAVE REPENTED OF YOUR SIN, DO YOU REALLY WANT TO FOLLOW CHRIST?
YES

NO

- IF YES, IT IS IMPORTANT TO MAKE APPOINTMENT WITH THEM.
- IF YOU ARE IN A HOME, YOU NEED TO ASK IF YOU CAN COME BACK AND TALK WITH THEM LATER.
- BE CAREFUL TO NOT WEAR YOUR WELCOME OUT
- DON'T BE PUSSHY.. PRAISE THEM FOR THE DECISION THEY HAVE MADE. SET A TIME AND DATE TO RETURN.

IT IS IMPORTANT TO FOLLOW UP

- BE CONSISTENT
- LET THE PERSON KNOW YOU CARE ABOUT THEM
- ASK IF YOU CAN PRAY WITH THEM
- DON'T BE IN A HURRY, DO NOT KEEP THEM TO LONG.

- GIVE THEM YOUR E-MAIL ADDRESS AND TELEPHONE NUMBER
- IF YOU ARE SOUL, WINNING AND YOU KNOW YOU CANNOT GET BACK TO SEE THEM...ASK IF YOU CAN HAVE A FRIEND CALL THEM OR E-MAIL THEM TO COME BY AND SEE THEM.
- REMEMBER, YOU ARE A NEW FACE AND THEY WILL NOT TRUST YOU AT FIRST. SO DO NOT BE PUSHY OR TO BOLD.

FOLLOW UP

- YOU SEND THEM A E-MAIL OR LETTER AS SOON AS POSSIBLE.
- YOU CAN CALL THEM ON THE PHONE AND ASK THEM HOW THEY ARE DOING. BUILD A FRIENDSHIP
- REMEMBER THE CULTS USE THIS PROCESS AND ARE VERY GOOD AT STEALING NEW CONVERTS.
- BEFORE YOU MAKE THE SECOND HOUSE CALL, CALL THEM AND ASK THEM TO WRITE DOWN ANY QUESTIONS THEY MAY HAVE.
- BE PATIENT AND CARING BUT, NOT OVER CARING.
- BRING WITH YOU INFORMATION ABOUT YOUR CHURCH
- ASK THEM IF THEY HAVE SEEN ANY CHANGES IN THEIR LIFE SINCE BECOMING A CHRISTIAN.
- SHOW THEM SCRIPTURE ACTS 8:26-38 THE STORY OF PHILIP AND THE EUNIC.. THIS IS A GREAT ICE-BREAKER FOR BAPTISM.

GREAT VERSES ON BAPTISM
- MT 3:7; MT 20:22-23; MT 21:25; MR 1:4; MR 10:38-39; MR 11:30; LU 3:3; LU 7:29; LU 12:50; LU 20:4; AC 1:22; AC 10:37; AC 13:24; AC 18:25; AC 19:3-4; RO 6:4; EPH 4:5; COL 2:12; 1PE 3:21

WHAT NEXT?

- BY NOW YOU HAVE MADE A FRIEND OR A ACQUAINTANCE.
- ASK THE PERSON IF YOU CAN MEET AGAIN WITH THEM.
- IF THE PERSON SAYS YES, YOU ARE ON YOUR WAY TO TRUE DISCIPLESHIP.
- ASK THEM IF THEY WOULD BE YOUR GUEST AT CHURCH AND MAKE SURE, YOU SIT WITH THEM WHEN THEY COME TO CHURCH.
- WHEN THE INVITATION IS GIVEN ASK IF THEY WOULD LIKE TO GO DOWN AND MAKE THEIR DECISION PUBLIC.

CHURCH MEMBERSHIP

- YOUR CHURCH HAS A CONSTITUTION AND IT IS IMPORTANT TO EXPLAIN WHAT IS REQUIRED AT YOUR CHURCH FOR MEMBERSHIP.
- ONCE THEY FOLLOW UP AND PUBLICLY, MAKE IT KNOWN THEY ARE A CHRISTIAN. SHOWING THEM THE BIBLICAL BASIS FOR MEMBERSHIP IS IMPORTANT.

David N. Smeltz

About the Author

Dr. David N. Smeltz was born in Lynchburg, Virginia during World War II. His parents were hard working people trying to make a life after the war. As a child, he lived in Allentown, Pennsylvania and at the age of seven, his family moved to Hialeah, Florida. He attended elementary, junior high and high school while residing in Florida. At age seventeen, he entered the Army and spent a little over one tour in Vietnam. After returning home from Vietnam in 1966, he went to work as a plumber and attended Junior College. In the fall of 1969, he met a young woman by the name of Susan Odell who invited him to church. While attending a revival in October 1969 he received Christ as his Savior and Lord. In February of 1970, he married Ms. Odell and they have been married for forty-four years. In 1973, he and his wife surrendered to the Gospel Ministry. He, his wife, and three children moved to Lynchburg, Virginia to attend Liberty Baptist College in 1974. After graduating from college in 1978, he and his family started Open Door Baptist Church in Halifax, Virginia. The church grew under his leadership to over 100 people with a Christian School and Day Care. In 1981, he assumed the pastorate of Fellowship Baptist Church in South Bend, Indiana. While there, he started a Christian School, Day Care, and Bible Institute and Citizens against Pornography. He assumed the leadership of Moral Majority for the state of Indiana in 1982 and worked with the Republican Party to elect Ronald Regan. He began working on his master's degree at New World Bible Institute. In 1985, he received his doctorate from Anchor Theological Seminary. He also attended J. Adams school of Christian Counseling and received his diploma in 1984. His pastorates have led him to New York, Washington State, Virginia and short time in Florida. He has pastored for 28 years served as a missionary evangelist for thirteen years at two different times. He has written

David N. Smeltz

eighteen books and many pamphlets. His ministry has led him to over 1000 churches in forty-one years of ministry preaching in many countries around the world. Both he and his wife travel together in a motor coach. They have five children, twelve grandchildren, and one great grandchild.

He has written four books on Islam and the most controversial of the three is the "The Great Deceiver" He is an accomplished gospel singer and has produced several gospel CD's. Most of his books can be purchase on Amazon.com both in paper back and Kindle.

To contact Dr. David N. Smeltz for bookings and meetings:
E-Mail pastor7777@hiswordoftruth.com
Web Site www.hiswordoftruth.com.

Made in the USA
Middletown, DE
26 March 2016